SAMSUNG GALAXY S25

Guidebook

A Practical Manual with Clear Step by step
instructions for Beginners and Advanced Users

Rhyan Baisten

TABLE OF CONTENTS

INTRODUCTION TO SAMSUNG GALAXY S25

The Samsung Galaxy S25 marks a new era of smartphone innovation, combining cutting-edge technology with sleek design and powerful performance. As the latest flagship in Samsung's renowned Galaxy S series, the S25 pushes the boundaries of what a smartphone can do, offering users an unparalleled experience in speed, camera capabilities, and AI-driven functionality.

The Samsung Galaxy S25 comes with smart AI features, a super-fast display, and an advanced camera to make work, creativity, and entertainment easier and better. Built with high-quality materials, strong security, and smooth connectivity, it's a perfect choice for both tech lovers and everyday users.

This guide will take you through everything you need to know about the Samsung Galaxy S25—from its stunning AMOLED display and powerful processor to its pro-grade camera system and next-gen AI enhancements. Whether you're upgrading from an older model or switching to Samsung for the first time, this book will help you unlock the full potential of your device and get the most out of your Galaxy S25.

CHAPTER 1

OVERVIEW OF THE SAMSUNG GALAXY S25

Samsung's Galaxy S25 series, unveiled in January 2025, represents the company's latest advancement in smartphone technology, emphasizing enhanced artificial intelligence (AI) integration and refined hardware design. The lineup includes the standard Galaxy S25, the S25+, and the flagship S25 Ultra, each catering to different user preferences.

A significant highlight of the Galaxy S25 series is its deep integration of AI capabilities. Collaborating with Google, Samsung has introduced a 'personal AI concierge' powered by advanced AI features. This system enables users to perform complex tasks across multiple applications through natural language commands, streamlining daily activities and reducing the need for manual app navigation. For instance, users can request the AI to compile information from various sources and present it cohesively, enhancing productivity and user experience.

In terms of performance, all models in the S25 series are equipped with the Qualcomm Snapdragon 8 Elite processor. This chipset delivers a 40% performance boost over previous generations, ensuring smooth multitasking and efficient handling of AI-driven features. The devices come with 12 GB of RAM, with storage options ranging from 128 GB to 1 TB, depending on the model. Notably, Samsung has committed to providing seven years of operating system and security updates for the S25 series, extending the devices' longevity and user value.

The Galaxy S25 series also showcases advancements in display technology. The S25 and S25+ feature Dynamic LTPO AMOLED 2X screens with a 120Hz refresh rate, offering vibrant visuals and smooth scrolling experiences. The S25 Ultra boasts a larger 6.9-inch display with enhanced brightness and clarity, making it ideal for media consumption and professional use. Design-wise, the S25 Ultra has been refined with more rounded corners and a titanium frame, providing both durability and a premium feel.

Camera capabilities have been a focal point in the S25 series. The S25 and S25+ are equipped with a 50-megapixel wide sensor, a 10-megapixel telephoto lens with 3x optical zoom, and a 12-megapixel ultrawide sensor. The S25 Ultra elevates this setup with a 200-megapixel wide sensor, a 50-megapixel periscope telephoto lens offering 5x optical zoom, and a 50-megapixel ultrawide sensor. These enhancements enable users to capture high-resolution photos and videos with improved detail and color accuracy.

Battery life is another area where the S25 series excels. The S25 Ultra, for example, is equipped with a 5,000 mAh battery, capable of providing up to 31 hours of video playback on a single charge. This endurance is complemented by fast charging capabilities, with the S25 Ultra supporting up to 45W wired charging and 25W wireless charging, ensuring users can quickly replenish their device's power as needed.

Key Features and Specifications

The Samsung Galaxy S25 boasts a sleek and upgraded design, featuring a powerful processor and long-lasting battery. This smartphone is designed for seamless gaming, multitasking, and photography experiences.

The phone comes with a large 6.8-inch Dynamic AMOLED display, ensuring vibrant visuals and smooth interactions. It is powered by the Exynos 2200 chipset and is equipped with 12GB of RAM to support demanding tasks. For storage, the device offers 256GB, with the option to expand via microSD, providing ample space for all your apps, media, and documents.

In terms of photography, the Galaxy S25 is equipped with an advanced camera setup, including a 50MP primary lens, a 10MP telephoto lens, and a 12MP ultra-wide lens. The front camera is a 12MP shooter, perfect for selfies and video calls.

The phone is powered by a 4000 mAh battery, which supports fast charging, ensuring that you spend less time plugged in and more time using your phone. It runs on the latest Android v15 operating system and supports 5G, Wi-Fi 6E, and Bluetooth 5.2 connectivity for faster and more reliable connections.

For added security, the Galaxy S25 features an in-display fingerprint scanner and face unlock capabilities, offering convenient and secure unlocking options. The dimensions of the phone are 146.9 x 70.5 x 7.2 mm, and it weighs 215 grams, making it comfortable to hold and use.

What's in the Box?

The box for the Galaxy S25 includes all the essential items you need to get started with your new device. Inside, you'll find the Galaxy S25 smartphone itself, ready to be powered up and used. Along with the phone, there is a USB-C cable that serves both for charging the device and transferring data. This cable ensures that your phone can be connected to other devices or a power source when necessary.

Also included is a SIM ejection tool, which is crucial for inserting or removing your SIM card, allowing you to access your network service. The package also contains paper inserts, which typically provide basic instructions or warranty information, guiding you through your initial setup.

This setup is consistent across the entire Galaxy S25 range, whether you've chosen the standard Galaxy S25, the larger S25 Plus, or the more feature-rich S25 Ultra. The only difference among these models is the phone itself, as each model offers different sizes and features, but the box contents remain the same. This simple packaging approach ensures you have the necessary tools to get your device up and running without extra clutter.

CHAPTER 2

GETTING STARTED

Setting Up Your Device

When you power on your Samsung Galaxy S25 for the first time, you may be guided through an initial setup process with a setup wizard. Here's how to get started:

To turn on your device, press and hold the Side key located on the side. Ensure that the battery is charged to at least 20% to allow the activation process to complete smoothly.

If prompted, enter your PIN code and select OK. If this doesn't appear, you can proceed to the next step.

Next, select your preferred language and tap Start. If prompted to restart, choose Restart, and the device will reboot automatically.

You'll then be asked to review and accept the Terms and Conditions. Select I agree to the Samsung Terms and Conditions, including the Dispute Resolution Agreement. You'll also need to accept the Samsung Privacy Policy.

You can choose to send diagnostic data to Samsung, but it's optional—if you agree, select Agree.

Now, you'll be given the option to set up the device manually—choose this option.

Your Samsung Galaxy S25 will scan for available Wi-Fi networks. Choose your preferred network. If your network isn't listed, ensure it's turned on and in range of the device. If prompted, enter your Wi-Fi password and tap Connect. Once connected, press Next.

You'll now have the option to skip transferring data—select Don't copy.

Next, you can log in with your email or phone number. Enter your email address, and if you don't already have a Google account, select Create Account and follow the instructions. Afterward, enter your Google account password and tap Next.

You'll be asked to scroll through and either agree or skip various terms and conditions—tap I agree.

For added security, you'll be asked to set up a screen lock. You can choose between PIN or fingerprint authentication. Set up your PIN or fingerprint, and follow the on-screen instructions to complete the setup.

If prompted, re-enter your screen lock code and choose OK, then tap Next. You'll be prompted to continue, select Continue, and then Register your fingerprint by following the instructions on the screen.

For fingerprint registration, place your finger on the fingerprint symbol and lift it off repeatedly until the scan is complete. Once registered, you may also choose to add more fingerprints if you wish, then tap Next.

If you wish to use face recognition, you can opt to register it now. Position your face in the camera frame and follow the on-screen instructions to complete the setup.

You may be given more options for privacy settings, such as sending usage and diagnostic data. Choose to turn them on or off as preferred. When finished, select Continue and confirm your settings.

At this stage, you'll also be able to choose backup settings, and password options, or set up later in the Settings menu. Once you are satisfied, select Confirm and Continue.

Finally, choose Home, and your Samsung Galaxy S25 will be ready for use!

Initial Configuration

Power On Your Device: Press and hold the Side button until the Samsung logo appears.

Insert SIM Card: If you haven't already, insert your SIM card into the device.

Select Language and Region: Choose your preferred language and region from the options provided.

Connect to Wi-Fi: Select your Wi-Fi network and enter the password to connect.

Agree to Terms and Conditions: Review and accept Samsung's terms to proceed.

Transfer Data (Optional): If you're switching from another device, you can transfer your data using Samsung's Smart Switch feature.

Sign in to Google Account: Enter your Google account credentials to access Google services.

Set Up Security Options: Choose a screen lock method, such as PIN, pattern, or password.

Samsung Account Sign-In (Optional): Sign in or create a Samsung account to access additional features.

Finalize Settings: Customize your device settings as desired.

TRANSFERRING DATA FROM YOUR OLD DEVICE

How to transfer using USB and WI-FI

1. **Install Smart Switch on Both Devices**:

   - For newer devices, go to **Settings > Accounts and Backup**, and look for **Smart Switch**.

- For older devices, download **Smart Switch** from the **Google Play Store**.

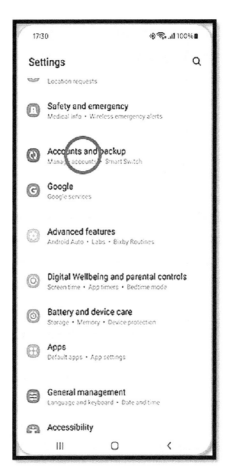

2. **Open Smart Switch on Your New Device**:

- On your new Galaxy S25, go to **Settings > Accounts and Backup**, and open **Smart Switch**.

- Tap **Bring data from the old device** under the **Smart Switch** options.

3. **Tap 'Receive Data':**

- In the **Smart Switch** app, tap on **Receive data** to start the process.

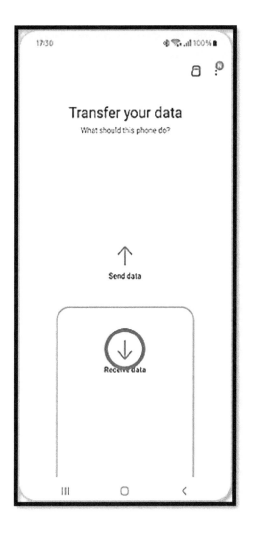

4. **Select 'Galaxy' or 'Android'**:

- Choose **Galaxy** if transferring from a Samsung device or **Android** if transferring from another Android phone.

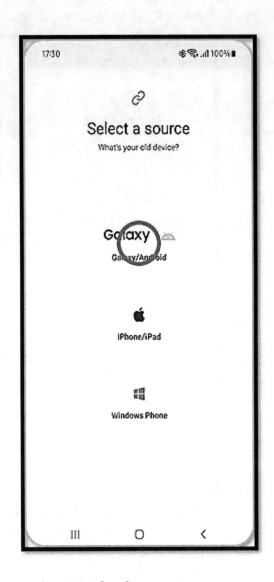

5. **Choose Connection Method**:

- **Wireless**: If using Wi-Fi, ensure the devices are close together and connected to a stable internet connection.

- **Cable**: If using a USB connection, plug the two devices together using the provided USB-C connector.

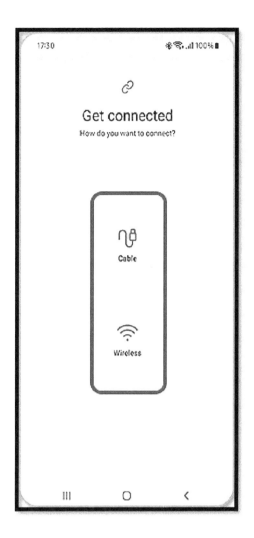

6. **Follow the On-Screen Instructions**:

- The transfer process will begin. You'll be prompted to choose which data (like contacts, apps, photos, etc.) you want to transfer.

- A progress bar will appear showing the percentage of data being transferred.

7. **Wait for the Transfer to Complete**:

- The time it takes will vary depending on the amount of data and the strength of your connection. Once the transfer is complete, your new Galaxy S25 will have all the selected data from your old device.

How to transfer using a PC or Mac

First, download Smart Switch onto your PC or Mac. Follow the on-screen instructions to install the software and open it.

Next, connect your old device to your computer. In the Smart Switch program, select the Backup option, then tap Allow on your phone to begin the process. Once the backup is finished, click OK and disconnect your old device.

Now, connect your new device to your PC or Mac. In the Smart Switch program, click Restore, then select Select a different backup and choose Samsung Device data.

You'll be able to deselect any data you don't want to transfer. Once you've made your selections, click OK, then choose Restore Now and tap Allow on your phone. The data transfer will begin.

Types of content that can be transferred through Smart switch

When transferring data, you'll have the option to select which types of content you want to move. However, there are certain limitations to what Smart Switch can transfer.

While most app data will transfer over, secure or encrypted data, such as WhatsApp chats, will not be moved. Many apps that require a username and password typically store data on their servers, so it's important to back up or save your information before logging into those apps on your new device.

Apps that were not downloaded from the Play Store will need to be manually re-downloaded. Smart Switch may also not be able to transfer login details for certain apps, like mobile banking. Be sure you have your login credentials ready for any apps you want to use on your new phone.

If you're transferring from an iOS device, note that the Google Play Store and the Apple App Store are separate, with different selections of apps and games. Smart Switch will attempt to download Android alternatives for the apps, but if an Android version is unavailable, that app won't be transferred.

Finally, content protected by Digital Rights Management (DRM) cannot be transferred through Smart Switch.

Inserting SIM and SD Card

To insert a SIM card into your Samsung Galaxy S25, you can use a SIM ejector tool or a paperclip to open the SIM card tray and insert the SIM card.

Here's how to do it:

1. Power off your phone.

2. Find the SIM card tray, usually located on the side of the phone.

3. Insert the SIM ejector tool or paperclip into the small hole next to the tray.

4. Gently press until the tray pops out.

5. Remove the tray from the phone.

6. Place the SIM card in the tray, ensuring the gold contacts are facing down.

7. Carefully slide the tray back into the phone.

8. Turn your phone back on.

Your SIM card is now installed and ready to use.

CHAPTER 3

NAVIGATING YOUR SAMSUNG GALAXY S25

HOME SCREEN BASICS

Home screen layout

To adjust the layout of your Samsung Galaxy S25 home screen, start by opening the Settings app. From there, navigate to the home screen settings, and locate the section labeled Home screen layout.

In this section, you will find two options for how you want your apps to be displayed. The first option is Home and Apps screens, which is the default setting. With this layout, your apps will be separated into two screens: the home screen for your most-used apps and an Apps screen where all other apps are stored. This allows you to keep your home screen tidy while still having access to all your apps on the app screen.

The second option is the Home screen only. When this setting is selected, all of your apps will be displayed directly on the Home screen, eliminating the separate Apps screen. This can give you quicker access to everything without needing to switch between different screens, but it may make the Home screen appear more cluttered.

Once you've selected your preferred layout, tap Apply to confirm your changes. Your home screen will now be organized according to the layout you choose, making it easier for you to navigate and personalize your device.

Home screen grid

To customize the home screen grid layout on your Samsung Galaxy S25, begin by opening the Settings app. Once in the settings, navigate to the section labeled Home screen, where you will find the option for Home screen grid.

This feature allows you to adjust the number of app icons displayed on your home screen by changing the grid layout. You will have several options to choose from, such as 4x5, 4x6, 5x5, or 5x6. Each option changes the arrangement of app icons, allowing you to have more or fewer icons visible depending on your preference. For example, selecting a 4x6 grid will display a smaller number of apps in larger icons, while a 5x6 layout will give you more apps in a tighter arrangement.

As soon as you select a grid layout, a preview of the change will appear above the options, allowing you to see how it will look on your home screen. Once you've decided on the layout you prefer, simply tap Done to apply the new home screen grid configuration. This change will immediately take effect, giving your home screen a fresh look and feel tailored to your needs.

Apps screen grid

To adjust the screen grid on your Samsung Galaxy S25, changing it to a higher setting, such as moving from 4x5 to 5x6, allows you to reduce the size of the app icons. This change helps conserve space on the screen and enables you to display more apps at once. This feature is only available when you're using the Home and Apps screens layout, which allows apps to be organized across two screens, the Home screen and the Apps screen.

To make this adjustment, begin by opening the Settings app. From there, navigate to the Home screen settings and select Apps screen grid. You'll then be presented with several grid options, such as 4x5, 4x6, 5x5, or 5x6, which refer to the number of rows and columns for the app icons. Choose the option that best suits your preferences, and once you make your selection, a preview of how the new layout will look will appear on the screen. After reviewing the preview, tap Done to apply the change.

If you want to further organize your Apps screen, you can also rearrange icons and remove any empty spaces. To do this, tap the Menu icon (the three-dot icon) on the Apps screen. From the options that appear, select Clean up pages to automatically remove any unused spaces between apps. Finally, tap Apply to confirm the changes. This will help streamline the App screen, making it more organized and easier to navigate.

Apps button

To manage the visibility of the Apps button on your Samsung Galaxy S25, you'll need to adjust the settings within the Home and Apps screens layout. This layout allows you to separate your most-used apps on the Home screen while keeping all other apps organized on the app screen.

To begin, open the Settings app on your device. Once inside the Settings menu, navigate to the Home screen section, where you'll find the option labeled Show Apps screen button on the Home screen. This setting controls whether the Apps button, which provides quick access to all your apps, will appear directly on your Home screen.

By toggling this option, you enable the Apps button, which will then appear on your Home screen for easy access to your full app list. If you prefer a cleaner Home screen and don't need the button, you can toggle the option off, and the Apps button will no longer be visible, leaving you with a more streamlined layout.

This simple adjustment gives you control over how you access and organize your apps, allowing you to either keep the Apps button accessible for quick navigation or remove it for a more minimalist approach to your Home screen.

Hide apps

To hide specific apps from appearing on your Samsung Galaxy S25's Home and Apps screens, you can adjust the settings to ensure those apps remain out of view without deleting them. This option is useful if you want to keep your screen organized or maintain privacy for certain apps.

To get started, open the Settings app on your device. Once inside the settings, navigate to the Home screen section, and then choose the option labeled Home screen again. In this section, you will see the Hide Apps on Home and Apps screens option, which allows you to select the apps you want to hide.

After tapping this option, you will be presented with a list of all the apps installed on your device. From this list, simply select the apps you wish to hide. Once you've made your selections, tap Done to apply the changes. The apps you've chosen will no longer be visible on either the Home screen or the Apps screen, but they are still installed on your phone and can be accessed in other ways, such as through the search function.

This feature is particularly useful if you want to keep your Home and Apps screens clean and uncluttered, while still retaining access to the hidden apps when needed.

Understanding the Touchscreen Gestures

Smartphone navigation has evolved significantly in recent years, and the Samsung Galaxy S25 takes this to the next level with its advanced gesture-based controls. Navigating your phone has never been more intuitive, thanks to the integration of modern Android gestures and touch commands. These gestures offer a more seamless and efficient way to interact with your device, making it easier to perform common tasks like switching between apps, going back to the home screen, or opening the recent apps menu.

The goal of these new navigation options is to make using your phone as smooth and user-friendly as possible. With the Samsung Galaxy S25, the days of traditional physical buttons are behind us, replaced by fluid gestures that respond to simple swipes and taps. Whether you're swiping up to access your apps, using a swipe gesture to go back, or navigating between tasks with a swipe of your finger, the experience feels natural and effortless.

This shift to gesture-based navigation reflects a broader trend in smartphone design, where the focus is on creating more efficient, intuitive user interfaces. The smart navigation system on the Galaxy S25 is designed to anticipate user behavior, making the entire experience feel more responsive and less cluttered. With this new approach, your interactions with the phone feel more connected and fluid, enhancing the overall experience. It's all about simplifying the way you use your phone and making everyday tasks more accessible and efficient with just a few swipes.

Traditional vs. Gesture Navigation

The way we navigate smartphones has significantly changed over the years. In the past, phones relied on physical buttons and specific touch controls to help users interact with their devices. These buttons were necessary to access key functions like the home screen, switching between apps, or going back to previous pages. While this setup was effective, it often felt more rigid and less fluid, as it required the user to rely on tactile buttons to perform actions.

With the introduction of modern gesture navigation, the user experience has become far more immersive and intuitive. Instead of needing to press a button for every action, you now simply swipe or tap in various directions to control the device. This system allows for more fluid movement between tasks. For example, you can effortlessly swipe between apps, allowing for smoother multitasking without needing to press physical buttons. Moving between screens, opening apps, or going back to the previous page now feels more natural, as the device responds directly to your touch.

Accessing the home screen is just as simple, with an easy motion that replaces the need for a dedicated home button. Similarly, switching between recent applications has been made much faster and more efficient. The gesture-based navigation system eliminates the need for extra steps, enabling you to seamlessly flow between tasks with a simple swipe or gesture. This evolution makes the user experience feel more connected to the device, offering a sense of fluidity and ease that wasn't possible with the older, button-based navigation methods.

Benefits of Using Swipe Gestures

The introduction of swipe gestures has greatly improved the overall smartphone experience, offering a variety of benefits that enhance how we interact with our devices. One of the primary advantages is that swipe gestures free up more screen space. With the removal of physical buttons or the need for on-screen navigation buttons, users gain more room to view content and interact with apps, allowing the screen to be used more effectively.

Swipe gestures also make interactions with the phone more intuitive. Instead of relying on pressing specific buttons or looking for on-screen icons, users can simply swipe in different directions to perform tasks. This natural motion feels more in tune with how we interact with technology, creating a smoother and more organic experience. For instance, swiping up to access apps or going back with a simple swipe feels more instinctive, reducing the need for users to memorize complex commands.

Another important benefit is that swipe gestures reduce the wear and tear on physical buttons. As fewer physical buttons are needed to perform tasks, the stress on the device's hardware is minimized, which can prolong the lifespan of the device. Physical buttons are often the first components to fail due to frequent use, and gesture navigation helps to mitigate this issue, providing a longer-lasting, more durable smartphone.

Overall, using swipe gestures leads to a better user experience. It streamlines how we navigate, making actions quicker and more seamless, and it aligns the device's functionality with modern expectations. Whether it's for multitasking, switching apps, or navigating through content, swipe gestures simplify these tasks, giving users a smoother and more satisfying experience when using their smartphones.

Activate Swipe Gestures on Galaxy S25

The Samsung Galaxy S25 comes equipped with an intuitive and advanced system of smart navigation gestures that enhance the way you interact with your phone. These gestures allow you to navigate through the device with simple swipes, making it easier and more efficient to access various features. By adjusting the default settings, you can tailor the gesture experience to suit your preferences and needs.

To activate swipe gestures and begin using them on your Galaxy S25, you'll need to make a few quick adjustments in the settings. The process is straightforward and designed to make your phone more responsive and user-friendly. Start by opening the Settings app on your device. From there, navigate to the Display section in the menu, where you will find options related to how the screen behaves. Tap on Navigation Bar, which is where you can adjust how you want to interact with the phone.

Under the Navigation Bar settings, select Swipe gestures to enable this feature. You will need to toggle the switch to activate full-screen gestures, allowing you to navigate the phone using simple swipe motions. Once activated, these gestures bring a new level of convenience. You can swipe up to return to the Home screen, swipe from the sides to go back, and swipe up and hold to access your recent apps. These gestures replace the need for physical buttons, offering a more modern and fluid way to interact with your phone.

What makes these gestures even more versatile is that you can customize them to better fit your individual preferences. The Samsung Galaxy S25 allows you to fine-tune these gestures through the Navigation settings, providing options to modify how the device responds to your swipes. Whether you prefer a more compact navigation bar or wish to adjust the sensitivity of certain gestures, the settings can be easily adjusted to match your usage style.

If you use the S Pen, you don't need to worry about compatibility. The Galaxy S25 is designed to work seamlessly with both touch gestures and the S Pen, allowing you to perform gestures with the stylus in the same way you would with your fingers. This ensures that whether you're using the touchscreen or the S Pen, the navigation system remains efficient and responsive, making the overall experience more intuitive and enjoyable.

Customizing Your Gesture Experience

The Samsung Galaxy S25 offers an advanced and personalized gesture experience that allows you to make navigation even more tailored to your preferences. Customizing the gestures enhances the overall ease of use, making the device feel more intuitive and responsive. By adjusting different aspects of the gesture settings, you can ensure that your interactions with the phone are smooth and effortless, perfectly fitting your unique usage style.

One of the key customization options is adjusting the sensitivity of gestures, which can significantly improve how the device responds to your touch. For instance, if you find that swipes don't register as smoothly or feel too sensitive, you can modify the sensitivity levels to make the experience more comfortable. This fine-tuning ensures that each swipe, tap, or hold feels natural, whether you're using the phone with one hand or performing more intricate gestures.

To adjust the gesture sensitivity, simply navigate to the settings on your Galaxy S25. Within the Settings app, head to Advanced Features and select Gestures. Here, you'll find options that allow you to customize how sensitive the gestures are to your touch. You can experiment with different levels of sensitivity to find what feels most comfortable for you, whether you prefer a more responsive gesture or a less sensitive one. This makes it easier to interact with the device in a way that fits your individual needs.

You can test and further customize how the device responds to specific gestures. For example, you might want the back gesture to register with less pressure or perhaps increase the sensitivity for switching between apps. The Galaxy S25 allows you to adjust these preferences individually, giving you full control over how each gesture behaves. This attention to detail makes the device more adaptable and user-friendly, ensuring that every action you take on your phone feels seamless and efficient.

Mastering One-Handed Mode

One-handed mode on the Samsung Galaxy S25 is a helpful feature, particularly for users who prefer using their phone with one hand or for those who find it challenging to reach across a larger screen. This mode reduces the size of the screen, making it more manageable and easier to interact with all parts of the display without needing to stretch your fingers. Whether you're replying to a message, navigating through apps, or just browsing, this feature ensures a more comfortable experience when using your device with limited hand mobility.

To enable one-handed mode on your Galaxy S25, simply go into the Settings app, where you'll find the option to activate this feature. Once turned on, you can adjust the size and positioning of the reduced screen to better suit your preferences. This allows you to move the shrunken screen to one side, so you can reach all areas with ease, making everyday tasks far more convenient.

The one-handed mode can be customized further by adjusting the gesture triggers, allowing you to access the feature quickly whenever you need it. For example, you can enable the ability to activate one-handed mode by swiping down from the corner of the screen or by using specific on-screen gestures. These options make it more efficient and faster to switch in and out of one-handed mode, depending on the situation.

Beyond resizing the screen, the Galaxy S25 also includes features like direct call gestures and palm swipe capture, which add extra convenience. The direct call gesture allows you to automatically dial a contact by bringing the phone to your ear, while the palm swipe capture feature enables you to take screenshots with a simple swipe of your hand. These functionalities work seamlessly within one-handed mode, further enhancing the multitasking experience and providing more flexibility as you use your device. This makes the Samsung Galaxy S25 not only easier to use but also more efficient for users on the go.

How to use the Now bar and Now brief features

The Samsung Galaxy S25, equipped with One UI 7, offers two powerful features called the Now bar and Now brief that help you stay informed without needing to unlock your phone. These features bring relevant updates directly to your lock screen, making it easier to stay connected to the things that matter most to you, all without interrupting your flow or unlocking the device.

The Now bar is a useful tool that allows you to view real-time information on your lock screen. This feature can display a variety of notifications, such as alerts about incoming messages, music playing, or the current mode or routine your phone is set to. With the Now bar, you don't need to open apps or unlock your device to check the latest updates or control basic features. It offers a convenient, glanceable way to access live data directly from the lock screen, streamlining how you interact with your device throughout the day.

To enable and customize the Now bar on your Galaxy S25, start by navigating to the device's settings. Once in the settings, look for the options under Lock Screen and enable the Now bar feature. You can choose what type of content you want to display in the Now bar, such as which notifications or media controls you would like to appear. This customization ensures that the information you need is always visible in the most convenient format, reducing the need to unlock your phone.

In addition to the Now bar, the Now brief feature offers a personalized, daily briefing that updates throughout the day with selected content. This feature is perfect for those who like to stay updated on a variety of things, such as news, reminders, or even weather information. The

Now brief is designed to give you quick insights into what's happening, whether it's the latest messages, appointments, or a glance at your upcoming schedule, all delivered in a way that feels customized to your preferences.

To use and set up the Now brief, you will need to go to the same Lock Screen settings where you enabled the Now bar. There, you'll find the option to activate Now brief and customize the specific types of content you want to be included in your daily briefing. You can select what matters most to you, such as daily reminders, news headlines, weather updates, or even fitness data. Once enabled, the Now brief will automatically update throughout the day, providing you with timely, relevant information, and allowing you to stay on top of things without needing to unlock your phone or open apps.

Both the Now bar and Now brief features on the Samsung Galaxy S25 enhance the lock screen experience by offering real-time, personalized updates. Whether it's through the Now bar's instant notifications or the Now brief's dynamic daily briefings, these features bring important content to your fingertips, making it easier to manage your day while keeping your phone organized and efficient.

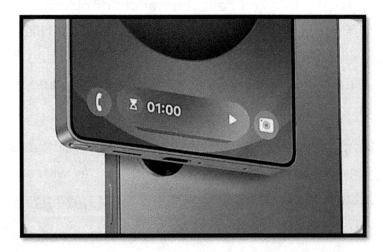

Customizing The Now Bar Features

The Now bar on your Samsung Galaxy S25 is a versatile feature that allows you to keep essential information visible directly on your lock screen. This feature enables you to view live notifications, music details, and modes or routines without unlocking your phone, offering a more streamlined and efficient way to stay connected with your apps and activities.

To customize the Now bar to suit your preferences, start by opening the Settings app on your Galaxy S25. From there, navigate to the Lock screen and AOD section, which controls various lock screen settings, including the Now bar.

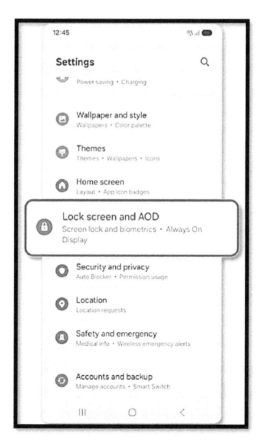

Once you're in this section, tap on the Now bar to access the customization options.

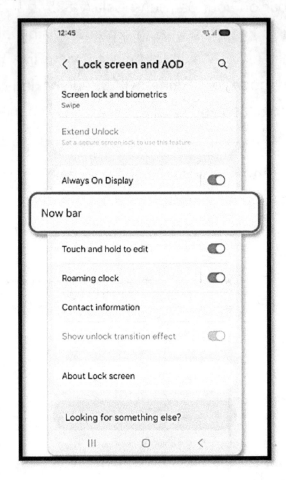

Here, you can select which types of information you want to appear in the Now bar. You will see a series of toggles that allow you to enable specific content, such as live notifications, music playback details, and your active modes or routines. By tapping the switches for the options you'd like to see, you ensure that your lock screen is filled with relevant, real-time data that you can check at a glance. If you want to explore additional options, you can tap View More, which will open more detailed customization choices.

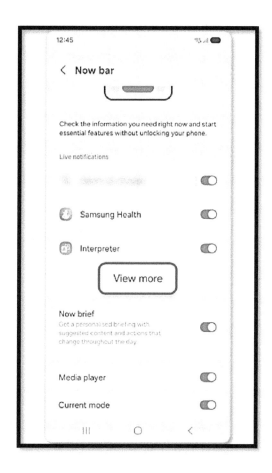

After enabling the desired content for the Now bar, the next step is to allow live app notifications to show up in the bar. This feature is particularly useful as it keeps you informed about incoming messages, app updates, or alerts without needing to unlock your phone or open apps. To activate live notifications, simply tap the switches to enable the relevant settings under the Now bar live notifications. Once activated, the notifications will appear on the lock screen, keeping you updated, while maintaining a clean and organized Home screen.

By customizing the Now bar, you can turn your lock screen into a highly functional, personalized information hub that suits your daily needs. This feature enhances your device's usability, giving you quicker access to the things that matter most without interrupting your tasks.

Using the Now Bar on the Lock Screen

The Now bar on the Samsung Galaxy S25 provides a convenient way to manage certain apps directly from your lock screen without needing to unlock the phone. This feature is particularly useful for controlling things like music playback, timers, or the stopwatch while you're on the go. It simplifies your experience by allowing you to interact with these apps quickly and easily, saving time and making multitasking more efficient.

To use the Now bar, begin by waking up your lock screen. You can do this by either double-tapping the screen or pressing the Power button. Once the lock screen is active, you'll see the Now bar, which may display live information depending on the apps you have running.

If the Now bar isn't immediately visible, you can swipe upward to access it, depending on the content that's currently being displayed.

Once the Now bar is in view, tap on it to open an expanded version that gives you more detailed controls over the apps you're interacting with. This expanded view allows you to manage the running apps more easily, providing a larger interface for controlling your music, adjusting a timer, or stopping a stopwatch.

If you want to access additional options, you can long-press the Now bar.

This action will open up further settings, such as the option to remove the bar from your lock screen or modify the Now bar settings to better suit your preferences. You have full control over what appears in the Now bar and how it functions, giving you the flexibility to customize it based on your needs.

However, it's important to note that the Now bar only appears when both lock screen notifications and app notifications are enabled. It will show up in real-time, but only when an app is open and actively running. This means the Now bar is designed to be a dynamic feature that updates as you use your device, ensuring that you have quick access to important information while maintaining a clean and organized lock screen.

Now Brief Feature

The Samsung Galaxy S25 offers a personalized and dynamic way to keep track of your day through the Now Brief feature. This feature provides brief, easy-to-digest cards that update throughout the day with relevant information tailored to your preferences. Whether it's reminders, news, weather updates, or upcoming appointments, the Now brief gives you a quick overview of the content you care about most, directly on your lock screen.

To personalize the content displayed in the Now brief, begin by opening the Settings app on your device. From there, navigate to Galaxy AI, a section where you can manage various smart features that enhance your user experience.

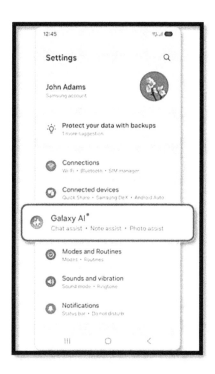

Once in the Galaxy AI settings, tap on Now Brief to access the options for customizing the content that appears in the briefing.

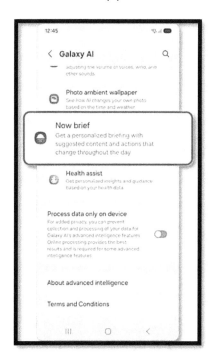

In the Now brief settings, you will find the option labeled Content to include. By tapping on this, you'll be able to select from a variety of content sources and types, allowing you to tailor the information you want to see.

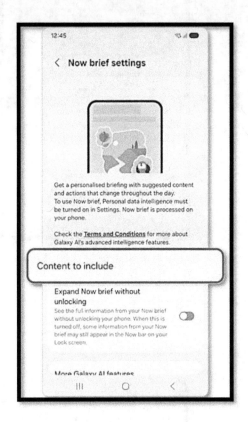

This could include things like your daily calendar events, weather updates, news headlines, or even fitness and health data. The beauty of the Now brief is that it pulls together all of these updates into compact, easy-to-read cards that refresh throughout the day, ensuring that you're always in the loop.

After selecting the content you'd like to include, the Now brief will automatically update based on the settings you've chosen. This allows you to have a personalized, real-time briefing of what's important to you, helping you stay organized and informed without having to dig through apps or notifications. The feature enhances convenience by bringing your most relevant information to the forefront, all without requiring you to interact with your device in a complicated way.

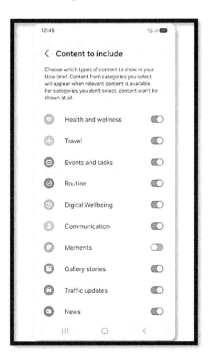

How to access Now brief through Edge Panel

Accessing the Now brief on the Samsung Galaxy S25 is simple and convenient, offering multiple ways to view your personalized content updates throughout the day. In addition to the notifications that appear on your lock screen via the Now bar, you can easily access the Now brief directly from your Home screen or through the Edge panel, making it even more accessible.

To access the Now brief through the Edge panel, first, swipe left from the top right of the screen. This gesture opens the Edge panel, which provides quick access to various tools, apps, and features, including the Now brief.

Once the panel appears, you'll see an icon for the Now brief. By tapping this icon, you will be taken directly to the Now brief, where you can view the latest updates and personalized content you've selected to display. This streamlined access through the Edge panel makes it quick and easy to stay updated without needing to unlock your phone or navigate through menus.

The Edge panel is a great feature because it allows you to access information with minimal effort, ensuring that your most important updates are always within reach. Whether you want a glance at your schedule, recent news, or weather forecasts, the Now brief gives you a snapshot of the day's relevant information, directly accessible from the Edge panel for your convenience.

Access from the Now Brief widget

Accessing the Now brief from the widget on your Home screen provides another easy way to stay informed throughout your day. The Now brief widget is designed to give you a quick, at-a-glance update of the personalized content you've chosen, such as your calendar events, weather, news, and more.

To use the Now brief widget, simply tap it on your Home screen. Once tapped, the content you've selected in the settings will appear immediately, giving you a live view of updates that are relevant to you. These updates refresh regularly, ensuring that the information you see is current, so you can stay on top of your day without needing to unlock your phone or navigate through multiple screens.

The beauty of using the Now Brief widget is its accessibility and efficiency. It allows you to view the information that matters to you, such as reminders or news headlines, with a simple tap. This feature keeps your most important updates visible and easily accessible, making your experience with your Samsung Galaxy S25 more streamlined and focused on what's relevant to you. Whether it's a glance at your schedule or a glance at the weather, the Now Brief widget ensures that you have the information you need right at your fingertips.

CUSTOMIZING THE HOME SCREEN

Add Apps

To add an app or a shortcut to a specific contact or bookmark to your Samsung Galaxy S25's Home screen, the process is simple and efficient. Adding shortcuts allows you to quickly access your favorite apps or contacts without needing to navigate through multiple screens.

To begin, find the app you wish to add to the Home screen. Once you've located it, touch and hold the app icon until a menu appears. This will give you the option to move the app icon or create a shortcut. Drag the app icon to the Home screen, or to the area where you want it placed.

For the app to be successfully added, ensure there is enough available space on your selected Home screen. If there isn't enough room, you can create additional Home screen panels by simply adding a new one. This will provide more space to arrange your apps and shortcuts in a way that suits your preferences.

It's important to note that adding shortcuts for individual contacts or bookmarks can only be done via widgets. These widgets allow you to place personalized shortcuts, making it quicker and easier to access your contacts or favorite websites directly from the Home screen.

By customizing your Home screen with apps and shortcuts, you can streamline your device's layout and enhance your efficiency in using your phone.

Add Widgets: are mini-apps (e.g., weather, clock, calendar, etc.)

Widgets are small applications, such as weather updates, clocks, or calendars, that provide quick access to important information directly from your Samsung Galaxy S25's Home screen. Unlike app shortcuts, which simply open the app, widgets display live data and often take up more space on the screen. This makes them ideal for users who want to keep essential information visible and easily accessible without opening an app.

To add a widget to your Home screen, start by pressing and holding a space on your screen. This action will bring up the option to customize the Home screen, including adding widgets. Tap on Widgets, and a list of available widgets will appear. From here, you can select the app whose widget you wish to add.

After selecting the desired widget, touch and hold it, then drag it to the Home screen where you'd like it to appear. Once you position the widget in the desired location, release it, and the widget will be added to your screen. It's important to ensure that there is enough space on the screen for the widget. If necessary, you can add more Home screen panels to create additional space.

Some widgets may offer additional customization options. If applicable, you can tap on these options to activate and configure the widget based on your preferences. The available options will vary depending on the type of widget, giving you the flexibility to adjust the display and settings to suit your needs.

By adding widgets to your Home screen, you can enhance your device's functionality, keeping important information readily available without needing to open multiple apps. This feature allows for a more streamlined and efficient user experience.

Changes to the appearance of widgets and app icons

The latest update to the Samsung Galaxy S25 brings a significant improvement to the appearance of widgets and app icons. In previous versions of One UI, when widgets and apps were placed side by side on the Home screen, they sometimes appeared misaligned because widgets did not have labels. This made the layout feel a bit disorganized and uneven, especially when organizing apps and widgets together.

With the introduction of labels for widgets in this new update, the alignment of widgets next to app icons is much more refined and polished. The labels add clarity, making it easier to identify each widget while creating a cleaner, more cohesive look on your Home screen. This change is especially noticeable when you have multiple widgets arranged next to app icons, as the labels help maintain a consistent and aligned aesthetic.

However, if you prefer a more minimalistic approach and want to display your widgets without labels, this option is still available. You can easily disable the labels by following a simple set of instructions. This allows you to return to the previous look, with the widgets appearing without any text beneath them. Whether you prefer the new, more organized style or the classic label-free layout, this update gives you the flexibility to customize the appearance of your Home screen to suit your preferences.

Turning labels on and off for both Apps and Widgets

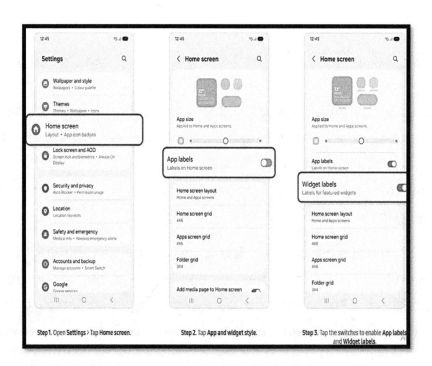

Step 1. Open Settings > Tap Home screen.   Step 2. Tap App and widget style.   Step 3. Tap the switches to enable App labels and Widget labels.

On your Samsung Galaxy S25, you have the option to adjust the size of the app icons on your Home screen. This customization allows you to make the icons larger or smaller based on your preferences, helping you achieve a layout that best suits your needs.

To change the app icon size, simply open the Settings app and navigate to the Home screen settings. Once there, you'll find a slider that allows you to adjust the size of the icons. By dragging the slider to the left, the icons will become smaller, allowing you to fit more apps on your Home screen. Moving the slider to the right will increase the size of the icons, making them more prominent and easier to tap.

This feature is great for those who want to personalize the layout of their Home screen, either for aesthetic reasons or for ease of use, depending on whether you prefer a more compact or spacious look for your apps.

Add / Remove Folders

Managing folders on your Samsung Galaxy S25 Home screen helps you organize your apps efficiently, making it easier to access them without cluttering your screen. Folders allow you to group related apps, so you can quickly find what you need.

To create a folder, start by touching and holding an app shortcut, such as your Email app. While holding the app, drag it over another app shortcut, like the Calendar app, and then release it. The two apps will now be grouped into a folder automatically. This helps to keep your Home screen tidy while still giving you quick access to the apps you use most.

If you want to give the folder a specific name, tap the default Folder name text at the top of the folder. This will open a field where you can enter a new name for the folder that better reflects the apps inside it, like Work or Social Media. After entering the name, simply tap Done to save your changes.

To remove a folder, drag any app out of the folder and place it on the Home screen. As soon as all the apps are removed, the folder will disappear automatically. This process gives you flexibility in customizing your Home screen as your app usage and preferences change over time.

By creating and managing folders, you can keep your apps neatly organized, reducing the clutter on your Home screen while maintaining easy access to the applications you need.

For the new update on your Samsung Galaxy S25, you now can expand the size of app folders on your Home screen. Previously, app folders were limited to a 1x1 size, which could sometimes make it difficult to see all the apps within the folder at a glance. Now, you can resize the folders to a 2x2 layout, providing a larger view of the apps grouped.

This change enhances the usability of your device, as it allows you to see more apps within a folder without having to open it up. The larger folder size makes it easier to quickly identify and access the apps you need, all with just a single tap. It also helps keep your Home screen organized while offering a more convenient way to manage your apps, making it simpler to find and open your most-used applications.

Whether you're grouping similar apps for quick access or just prefer a more spacious layout, this new folder size option offers flexibility and improved efficiency in how you organize your device.

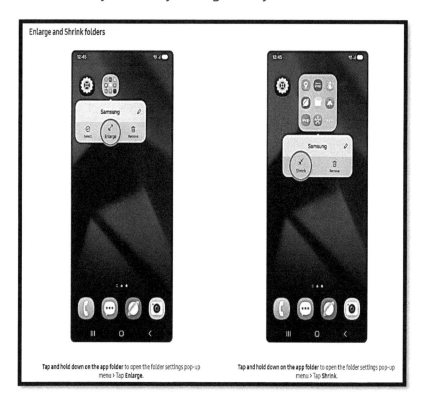

Tap and hold down on the app folder to open the folder settings pop-up menu > Tap **Enlarge**.

Tap and hold down on the app folder to open the folder settings pop-up menu > Tap **Shrink**.

Remove Apps / Widgets

Removing apps or widgets from the Home screen of your Samsung Galaxy S25 is a straightforward process that allows you to customize your device's layout by getting rid of items you no longer need or use.

To begin, locate the app or widget you wish to remove. Press and hold the item, such as a shortcut or widget, until a menu appears. Once the menu pops up, simply release your finger. The menu will display an option to Remove the item from the Home screen.

By tapping Remove, the selected app or widget will be removed from the screen, but it will not be deleted from your device. If it's an app, it will still be available on your Apps screen, and if it's a widget, it will still be accessible through the widgets menu.

This feature is particularly useful for decluttering your Home screen, allowing you to keep it organized and only showing the apps and widgets that are most important to you.

Set Wallpaper

Changing the wallpaper on your Samsung Galaxy S25 allows you to personalize your device and make it feel uniquely yours. Whether you want to use a pre-loaded wallpaper or an image from your gallery, the process is easy to follow.

To begin, touch and hold any blank space on your Home screen. This action will open a menu, where you can select Wallpaper and Style located in the lower-left corner. Once selected, tap on Change Wallpapers to proceed.

If you prefer to use a pre-existing wallpaper, you can choose from several categories, such as Featured, Creative, Graphical, or Colors. These options display a variety of wallpapers that are readily available. Browse through the choices, and once you find one you like, tap on it. If prompted, choose whether you want the wallpaper to be applied to your Home screen, Lock screen, or both. After selecting your preference, tap Next and then Done to set the wallpaper.

Alternatively, if you want to use a photo from your gallery, tap on Gallery. This will open your photo library, where you can browse and select your desired image. You can select up to 15 images, which will be displayed in a rotating slideshow. Once you've chosen your image(s), tap Done. If you're asked, select whether the image should be applied to your Home screen, Lock screen, or both. If you select multiple pictures, the changes will only apply to the Lock screen. You can also adjust how the image is displayed, such as resizing or repositioning it to fit your screen, before tapping Done to finalize the change.

By customizing your wallpaper, you can give your phone a fresh look and feel, whether you prefer a static image or a rotating slideshow of your favorite photos.

One swipe access to the notification and quick settings panel

On your Samsung Galaxy S25, accessing both the notification and quick settings panels has become more efficient with a single swipe from the Home screen. This update allows you to easily manage notifications and adjust settings with just one swipe, enhancing the user experience by making it faster and more intuitive.

The swipe area for both panels is divided into a 7:3 ratio. This means that the majority of the swipe area is allocated to the notification panel, while a smaller portion is reserved for the quick settings panel. This design ensures that you can quickly check your notifications with a simple swipe, while still having easy access to your quick settings, such as Wi-Fi, Bluetooth, and Do Not Disturb.

 If the default swipe areas don't feel comfortable or natural to you, there's an option to adjust the position of the touch area for both the notification and quick settings panels. This customization allows you to fine-tune how you interact with your device, ensuring that the swipe gestures are intuitive and suit your personal preferences. By changing the position, you can make the experience more seamless, whether you prefer a larger notification panel or a more prominent quick settings section.

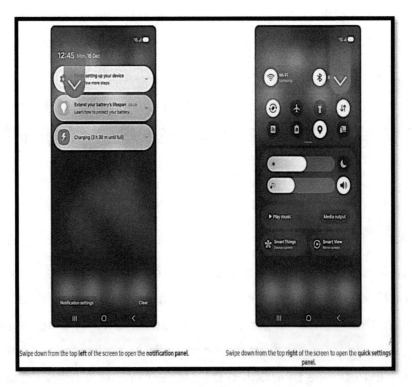

Swipe down from the top **left** of the screen to open the **notification panel.**   Swipe down from the top **right** of the screen to open the **quick settings panel.**

CHAPTER 4

ESSENTIAL SETTINGS AND CUSTOMIZATION

MANAGING DISPLAY AND BRIGHTNESS

Adjust the brightness

To adjust the brightness on your Samsung Galaxy S25, begin by opening the Settings app on your device. Once inside the Settings menu, tap on Display to access all the display-related settings, including brightness options.

In the Brightness section, you'll see a slider that allows you to control the brightness level of your screen. By sliding the blue bar left or right, you can decrease or increase the brightness according to your preference. If you find yourself needing more brightness during the day or in well-lit environments, simply slide the bar to the right. For darker environments or when you want to conserve battery, sliding the bar to the left will lower the brightness.

You can activate Adaptive brightness, a feature that adjusts the screen's brightness automatically based on the lighting conditions around you. When this option is turned on, your phone will continuously optimize the brightness for the current environment. If you prefer more control over the brightness settings and want to adjust it manually, you can turn off Adaptive brightness at any time.

By adjusting these settings, you can ensure that your screen is always comfortable to use, whether you're indoors, outside, or in varying light conditions. The Samsung Galaxy S25's flexible brightness options provide a more personalized viewing experience, making it easier to read and interact with your device.

Adjust Display / Font Settings

Customizing the display and font settings allows you to make your device's text and screen more tailored to your preferences, ensuring a comfortable viewing experience that suits your needs. To begin, access the Display settings by opening the Settings app on your phone.

Once you're in the Display settings, tap on Font size and style. In this section, you can easily adjust the font size to your liking. By touching and holding the blue dot on the slider, you can drag it left to decrease the font size or right to increase it. This gives you full control over how large or small the text appears on your screen.

Next, you can change the font style by tapping on Font style. Here, you'll be able to select from a variety of font options, such as Default, Samsung, and others, depending on your visual preference. After selecting a style that you like, tap the Back arrow to return to the Font size and style settings.

For those who prefer more prominent text, you can enable Bold font by toggling the switch on or off. This feature makes the text appear bolder, enhancing readability, especially in certain lighting or for users with visual impairments. When you're finished adjusting the font settings, tap the Back icon to return to the Display settings screen.

Another important setting is Screen timeout, which determines how long your screen stays on before it automatically turns off to save power. By tapping on Screen timeout, you can choose from several options, such as 15 seconds, 30 seconds, and so on. This allows you to customize the duration based on your usage habits.

If you want to control what happens when your phone is charging, tap Screen Saver. Here, you can select various options such as Colors, Photo Table, or other options that will display while your phone is charging, adding a personal touch to the idle screen. After making your selection, you can tap the Back icon to return to the Display settings screen.

Lastly, Screen zoom allows you to adjust how elements are displayed on the screen, making it easier to read or navigate. By tapping Screen Zoom, you can adjust the slider by touching and holding the blue dot and dragging it to the desired setting. This feature enables you to increase or decrease the size of icons and text to match your comfort level.

These display and font settings on the Samsung Galaxy S25 give you complete control over your phone's appearance, ensuring that it fits your visual needs and provides a personalized, comfortable experience.

Setting Up Security Options (Face ID, Fingerprint, Passcode)

Set up and use fingerprint unlock

Setting up fingerprint unlock on your Samsung Galaxy S25 enhances the security of your device while offering the convenience of quickly unlocking it with just a touch of your finger. The process is simple and nearly identical across devices, with the only difference being the location of the fingerprint sensor, which can vary depending on the model.

To get started, first, navigate to the Settings app on your device. From there, tap on Security and Privacy to access the relevant settings for securing your phone. Next, tap on the Lock screen, and then select Fingerprints from the list of options available. At this point, you'll be asked to enter your current lock screen credentials, such as a PIN, password, or pattern. If you haven't set up a screen lock yet, the device will prompt you to create one before proceeding. This is an important step as it ensures that your fingerprint data is protected.

Once you've entered your credentials, you'll see a brief informational screen about fingerprint registration. After reading the information, tap Continue to move on. Now, you'll need to register your fingerprint. Tap Register, and follow the on-screen instructions to begin the registration process. When registering your fingerprint, make sure to place your finger fully on the fingerprint sensor, covering it completely. It's important to avoid letting strong light interfere with the sensor during this process, as this could impact its ability to capture a clear scan of your fingerprint. Continue following the prompts until the device has successfully registered your fingerprint. When finished, tap Done.

After registration, ensure that the switch next to the Fingerprint unlock is turned on. This ensures that the fingerprint unlock feature is enabled, allowing you to unlock your phone using your registered fingerprint. If the fingerprint sensor is located on the Side button or beneath the Side button, you have the option to disable the Fingerprint always-on feature. Disabling this setting helps prevent accidental unlocks by ensuring the sensor only activates when you intentionally place your finger on it.

To unlock your device using fingerprint security, simply tap the screen or press the Power or Side button to wake the device. Then, place the finger you registered on the fingerprint sensor. If the device recognizes your fingerprint, it will automatically unlock, allowing you to access your phone quickly and securely. This convenient method not only enhances security but also streamlines the process of unlocking your device.

Once your fingerprint data is registered, review the security options and settings:

Once you've successfully registered your fingerprints, it's important to review and customize the security options to ensure that the device works in a way that best suits your preferences. These settings give you control over how fingerprint recognition functions, allowing you to personalize the feature for convenience and enhanced security.

If you wish to rename any of the fingerprints you've registered, simply tap on the desired fingerprint entry. You'll then be prompted to enter a new name for the fingerprint, which can be anything from your name to a more descriptive label, like Right Thumb or Left Index. After entering the new name, just tap Save to confirm the change.

Should you decide to remove a fingerprint from your device for any reason, the process is equally simple. Tap the fingerprint entry you want to delete and select Remove. This action will delete the fingerprint data from your phone, ensuring that it no longer has access to your device.

The option to Add fingerprints allows you to register up to four fingerprints in total, which is useful for registering both hands or different fingers, enhancing accessibility. This flexibility ensures that you can unlock your phone with whichever finger is most convenient at the time. Once added, you can test the recognition of your registered fingerprints to verify that the device accurately identifies them. This step ensures that the fingerprint sensor is working as expected and that your fingerprints are registered correctly.

The key feature is Fingerprint unlock, which is the core functionality allowing you to unlock your device when your fingerprint is detected. This provides an easy and secure way to access your phone, ensuring that only registered fingerprints can unlock the device. Additionally, the Fingerprint always-on option allows the fingerprint sensor to be active even when the screen is off, making it even more convenient to unlock your phone without needing to wake it first.

The Show icon when the screen is offsetting lets you decide when the fingerprint icon appears on the screen, providing visual cues for when you're ready to scan your finger. You can choose for the icon to be always displayed on the Always On Display, tap to show when you need it, or never show the icon if you prefer a cleaner look.

For a more interactive experience, the Show animation when unlocking option enables a fun and visual animation whenever you unlock your phone using your fingerprint, providing a more dynamic experience.

The About fingerprints section offers helpful tips for using the fingerprint feature effectively, guiding you on how to get the best results from fingerprint recognition.

It's important to note that if your device has been restarted or hasn't been used for more than 24 hours, you'll need to use your PIN, password, or pattern to unlock your phone instead of relying on your fingerprint. This added security measure ensures that even if your phone is restarted or idle for a long period, unauthorized access is prevented.

Add additional fingerprints

Adding multiple fingerprints can make it more convenient to unlock your device from different angles or when using a different hand. This feature is particularly useful when you're holding your phone in your left hand instead of your right, or if you want to ensure you can unlock your device regardless of how it's positioned. By registering additional fingerprints, you ensure greater flexibility and ease of use.

To add another fingerprint, start by navigating to the Settings app on your device. From there, tap on Security and Privacy, which will lead you to the various security options available. Next, tap on the Lock screen, then select Fingerprints to proceed to the fingerprint settings. At this point, you will be prompted to enter your secure screen lock credentials, such as a PIN, password, or pattern, to ensure that only you can add or modify fingerprints.

Once your credentials are entered, you'll see the option to Add a fingerprint. Tap this option, and the system will guide you through the registration process. Follow the on-screen instructions, which will ask you to place your finger on the fingerprint sensor multiple times to ensure a clear and accurate scan. The device will prompt you to adjust your finger position slightly each time to capture different parts of your fingerprint for a more complete registration. After successfully adding the new fingerprint, tap Done to finish the process.

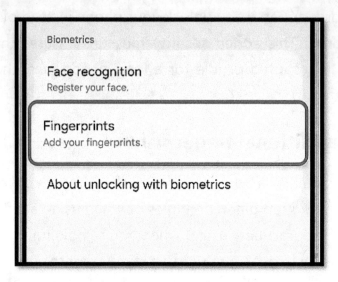

By registering multiple fingerprints, you ensure that no matter how you hold your phone, whether it's in your left or right hand, you can easily unlock it with a finger that feels most natural. This added convenience not only enhances security but also makes it faster and easier to access your device, especially when you're on the go.

Remove a fingerprint from your device.

If you no longer need a fingerprint registered or if you want to enhance your security by removing old fingerprints, the process is straightforward. It's important to note that if you remove all registered fingerprints, the Fingerprint unlock feature will be turned off by default, meaning you'll need to use an alternative method to unlock your device, such as a PIN, password, or pattern.

To begin, open the Settings app on your phone and navigate to Security and Privacy. From there, tap on the Lock screen, and then select Fingerprints to access the fingerprint settings. At this point, you will be asked to enter your security credentials, such as your PIN, password, or pattern, to verify that it's you making the change.

Once you have entered your credentials, you will see a list of the fingerprints that are currently registered on your device. Choose the fingerprint you wish to remove, for example, Fingerprint 1. Tap on it, and then tap the Remove button. The system will ask you to confirm your decision, so tap Remove again to finalize the process.

Removing a fingerprint is the same on all Android devices running version 9.0 or higher, regardless of the fingerprint sensor's location. This ensures that the process is consistent across various devices, making it easier for users to manage their fingerprint security settings. After successfully removing a fingerprint, the device will no longer recognize it for unlocking, but you can always add a new fingerprint later if needed.

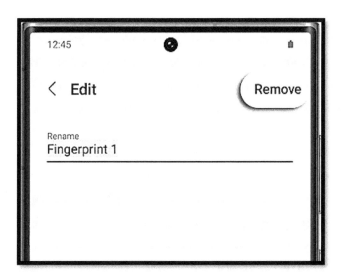

Trouble unlocking device with fingerprint

If you're having trouble unlocking your Samsung Galaxy S25 with the fingerprint sensor, there are a few things you can try to ensure it works smoothly. First, it's essential to make sure you're covering the entire sensor with your finger, as a partial touch can prevent the sensor from reading your print accurately. When using your fingerprint, try holding your device the same way you did when you initially registered your prints, as a slight change in grip could affect recognition.

Another important consideration is the cleanliness of both your finger and the fingerprint sensor. Make sure both are clean and dry before scanning your finger, as dirt, oil, or moisture can interfere with the sensor's ability to read your fingerprint. If necessary, wipe both the sensor and your fingertip gently before attempting to unlock your device again.

If the issue persists, try restarting your device. Sometimes, a quick reboot can resolve temporary software glitches that may be affecting fingerprint recognition. After restarting, give the fingerprint sensor another try to see if it now works properly.

Keeping your device and apps up to date is also crucial for optimal performance. Software updates often contain bug fixes and improvements that can enhance the functionality of features like fingerprint unlocking. If you're experiencing repeated issues, check for any available updates and install them.

If none of these solutions work, consider removing the registered fingerprints and re-adding them. This can help ensure that the fingerprints are stored correctly and eliminate any potential issues with the initial registration. After re-registering your fingerprints, try unlocking your device again.

If you're still unable to unlock your phone with your fingerprint, use your regular PIN, password, or pattern as a fallback method. This ensures that you can still access your device even if the fingerprint sensor isn't recognizing your prints at the moment. By following these steps, you can troubleshoot and resolve most issues with fingerprint unlocking, ensuring a smoother and more reliable user experience.

Set Up Face Unlock

To set up Face Unlock, start by opening the Settings app. Scroll down until you find the Security and Privacy section, then tap on Screen Lock and Biometrics under the Additional Security Settings category. At this point, you'll be asked to enter your current PIN, password, or pattern to verify your identity. If you haven't set one up yet, you'll be prompted to create one.

For extra security, you'll also need to set up an alternative unlock method, such as a PIN, password, or pattern. This ensures that you can still access your device if Face Unlock isn't available or if it fails for any reason. Once that's done, go back to the Screen Lock and Biometrics settings and select Face Recognition under the Biometrics section to start the setup process.

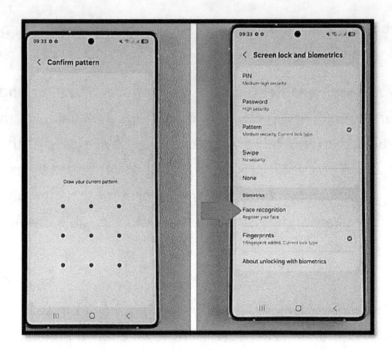

Tap Continue to start the setup process, then choose Register after reviewing the instructions to begin configuring your face recognition.

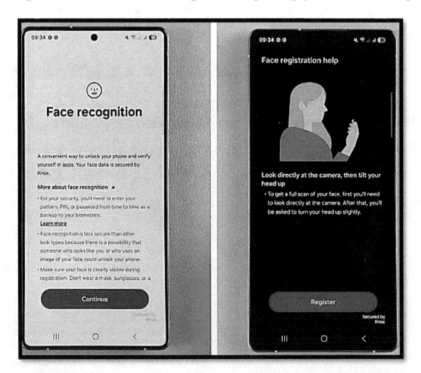

Follow the on-screen prompts to register your face. Hold your device at eye level and look straight into the camera, ensuring your face is within the designated circle. For the best results, tilt your face slightly upwards. The Galaxy S25 will capture several facial features to ensure accurate recognition. If you're wearing glasses, you might need to take them off during the process for better recognition.

After completing the enrollment process, you'll receive a confirmation letting you know that your face has been successfully registered. The Face Unlock feature will be enabled automatically, allowing you to unlock your Galaxy S25 with Face Recognition.

In the Face Recognition settings, you also have the option to tap on Add Alternative Appearance. This lets you add additional facial data to improve the accuracy of the recognition, making the unlocking process even smoother.

Connecting to Wi-Fi and Bluetooth

To connect to a Wi-Fi network, swipe up from the home screen to access your apps.

Once you've done that, tap on Settings. From the Settings menu, select Connections and then tap on Wi-Fi. This will bring up a list of available Wi-Fi networks.

Select Connections and then tap on Wi-Fi. This will bring up a list of available Wi-Fi networks.

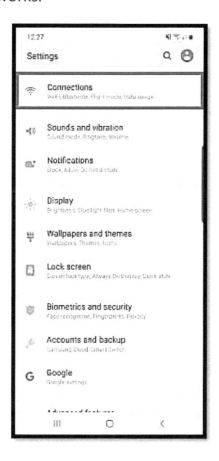

Find and tap on the Wi-Fi network you wish to join. Keep in mind that the network name, or SSID, is usually set when the network is configured. For many routers, the network name can be found printed directly on the router. If you're having trouble remembering the name of your network, it's a good idea to contact your Wi-Fi provider for assistance.

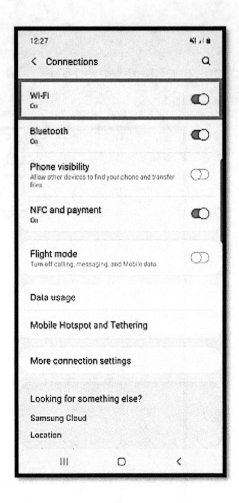

If the network is secured with a password, you'll need to enter it when prompted. The password is typically set during the network setup process, and for most routers, it can be found printed on the device itself. If you're struggling to recall your Wi-Fi password, you may need to reach out to your network provider for help.

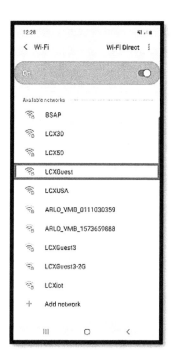

Once you've entered the password, you'll see an option to enable Auto-reconnect, which, when turned on, will automatically connect your device to this network in the future.

If you prefer not to have your device connect automatically, leave this option turned off.

Finally, tap Connect to establish your connection to the Wi-Fi network. Your device will then connect to the network, and you should be all set to start browsing.

Set up Bluetooth tethering.

To set up Bluetooth tethering start by swiping up from the home screen to open your apps. Then, tap on Settings, followed by Connections, and select Bluetooth.

Next, tap the device you want to connect to. Make sure the other device is in pairing mode, which is usually activated by opening its Bluetooth settings. If you're unsure, check the user guide for that device for more details.

Once both devices appear, tap OK on each device to confirm the connection.

After that, tap the back arrow to return to the main settings screen. From there, go to Mobile Hotspot and Tethering, and tap the switch next to Bluetooth tethering to enable it. Then, tap Bluetooth tethering to continue.

Next, on the connected device, tap the settings icon, followed by Internet access. An icon will appear in the notifications bar to indicate that Bluetooth tethering is now active.

When you're done using Bluetooth tethering, simply tap the switch to turn it off. You can also turn off Bluetooth entirely on your phone to disconnect the tethering feature.

Configuring Notifications and Do Not Disturb

For you to properly manage the Do Not Disturb feature on your Samsung Galaxy S25, begin by opening the Settings app. From there, navigate to Notifications, and then select Do not disturb. This will bring you to the settings where you can control when and how you want your phone to mute notifications and alerts.

If you want to immediately turn Do Not Disturb on or off, simply tap the switch at the top of the screen. This will activate or deactivate the feature instantly. If you'd prefer to set up a schedule, you can tap the switch next to an existing schedule to turn it on or off based on the times you've previously set.

To create a new schedule, tap Add Schedule. This will allow you to customize the days and times when you want Do Not Disturb to be active, ensuring that notifications are silenced during specific periods, like while you're sleeping or during meetings.

If you want to adjust an existing schedule, simply tap the schedule name and modify the settings as desired. You can change the days, start time, and other preferences to fine-tune your schedule.

In the Allowed During Do Not Disturb section, you can manage which types of notifications will still come through while the feature is activated. Tap on Calls and messages to adjust these settings. For calls, you can choose from options like All calls, Contacts only, or other preferences to decide which calls can get through. You can also enable the Repeat callers to switch to allow calls from the same person if they call twice within a short period.

For messages, you can similarly adjust the settings. Choose whether you want all messages or just those from contacts to be allowed through while Do Not Disturb is active.

Under Alarms and Sounds, you can control whether sounds and vibrations are muted for certain activities. Tap the items you want to adjust, such as Alarms, Media sound, or Touch sound, and toggle them on or off according to your needs.

By customizing the Do Not Disturb settings, you can ensure that your phone works around your schedule, allowing you to stay undisturbed while still receiving important calls, messages, or alerts when necessary.

CHAPTER 5

USING SAMSUNG APPS

How to Disable and Enable

On your Samsung Galaxy S25, some pre-installed apps, such as the Calculator or Google Play Store, cannot be uninstalled. However, if you're looking to free up space or reduce clutter on your device, you have the option to disable these apps instead. Disabling an app prevents it from running in the background and removes it from your app drawer, giving you more space and resources, although it's important to note that disabling certain apps could affect the functionality of related apps.

To begin, open the Settings app on your phone. From the settings menu, tap on Apps to access the list of applications installed on your device. If you need to see all apps, including system apps, tap on the Filter and Sort icon and select All to display every app on the device. If you still don't see the system apps, you may need to tap Show system apps to make them visible.

Once you have access to the full list of apps, you can choose to disable one by selecting the app you want to modify. After tapping on the app, you'll be presented with several options. If the app can be disabled, tap the Disable button, and then confirm by tapping Disable app. Disabling the app will stop it from running and remove it from your device's active list.

If you don't see the option to disable the app, you can try tapping on Force Stop instead. This action will immediately stop the app from running, though it doesn't disable it completely. After tapping Force Stop, confirm the action by selecting OK.

In some cases, you may be prompted to replace the app with its factory version. This usually happens when a system app has been updated or modified in some way. If prompted, tap OK to restore the app to its original state.

Disabling apps can be a helpful way to manage the apps on your device without fully removing them, allowing you to keep your phone running smoothly and efficiently. However, it's essential to keep in mind that some disabled apps might affect the behavior of other apps that depend on them. Therefore, it's always a good idea to check how your device functions after disabling certain apps to ensure everything works as expected.

Enable Apps

If you have previously disabled an app on your Samsung Galaxy S25 and now wish to enable it again, the process is simple. First, open the Settings app on your device. From the settings menu, navigate to Apps to view the list of installed applications. You can use the search feature or scroll through the list to find the specific app that you want to enable.

Once you locate the app, tap on it to open the app's settings. If the app has been disabled, you will see the Enable option. Simply tap Enable, and the app will be reactivated on your device. Once enabled, the app will return to its regular function, and it will once again appear in your app drawer, allowing you to use it as you would any other app.

Enabling an app is a quick way to restore functionality if you've disabled it temporarily, either to free up resources or reduce clutter. After enabling the app, it will be available for regular use, just like before.

Samsung Health and Samsung Pay

Samsung Pay offers a simple and efficient way to complete your purchases at a variety of stores, eliminating the need to carry physical credit or debit cards. Accessing Samsung Pay on your Samsung Galaxy S25 is a quick process, with several methods available to open the app, making it easy for you to use when you're ready to check out.

To open Samsung Pay, start by swiping up from the bottom of your phone's screen to access the app screen. Once you're there, look for the Samsung Pay app icon and tap on it to launch the app. This will bring up your payment options, allowing you to make quick, secure transactions.

If you've set up the Quick Access shortcut, you can launch Samsung Pay even faster. Just swipe up from the bottom of the screen, and Samsung Pay will open directly, ready for you to complete your payment. This feature is designed for convenience, providing an even quicker way to access the app without needing to navigate through your home screen.

 If you find that Samsung Pay is opening unintentionally due to the Quick Access shortcut, it can be easily disabled. To do so, open Samsung Pay and tap the Menu icon, represented by three horizontal lines. From the menu, select Settings, then choose Quick Access. Here, you'll find the option to toggle the switch off, which will prevent

Samsung Pay from launching automatically when you swipe up from the bottom of your screen. This way, you can maintain more control over when the app opens, ensuring it only launches when you want to use it.

Galaxy Store vs. Google Play Store

The Galaxy Store and Google Play Store are both app stores that offer Android apps, but they have some key differences.

	Galaxy Store	Google Play Store
Exclusive apps	Includes Samsung-exclusive apps like Samsung Wallet and Samsung Health	Includes apps for every Android phone, including Samsung
Content	Offers apps, discounts, and in-app promotions	Offers apps, games, books, movies, TV shows,

		and device updates
Updates	Some say it's faster at downloading and applying updates	Apps can't be auto-updated from Galaxy Store

You can install apps from both stores, but you might need to update an app from the same store.

Additional information about the Galaxy Store and Google Play Store:

- The Galaxy Store is Samsung's exclusive app store for Galaxy customers.

- The Google Play Store comes preinstalled on all Samsung smartphones.

- The Play Store app is usually located on your home screen.

- The Galaxy Store offers in-app promotions, including special banner ads and exclusive video notifications.

CHAPTER 6

CAMERA AND PHOTOGRAPHY TIPS

CAMERA FEATURES AND MODES

Lunch the Camera App

There are several convenient methods for quickly opening the Camera app. This allows you to capture moments instantly without navigating through multiple screens.

One way is from the Home screen, where you can simply tap the Camera icon to launch the app. This is the simplest approach if the Camera app is already placed on your home screen for easy access.

If your phone is locked, you can still access the Camera app without unlocking your device. On the Lock screen, swipe up from the camera shortcut icon. This feature allows you to open the Camera immediately, which is particularly useful when you don't want to unlock your phone just to take a quick photo.

Another method is through the Apps screen, where you can find the Camera app icon. By navigating to the Apps screen and tapping on the Camera icon, you can open the app just as you would any other app on your device.

If you prefer a faster approach, you can set up the Double press the Side button feature. This method allows you to launch the Camera app by double-pressing the Side button on your device. However, this option needs to be enabled first. To set it up, go to Settings, tap Advanced Features, and then tap the Side button. From there, select Double press, and toggle the switch to turn it on. After that, select

Camera to ensure the camera app opens when the Side button is pressed twice.

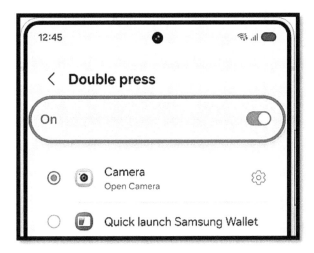

These various methods provide flexibility in how you access the Camera app, making it easier to capture photos whenever you need them, no matter the situation or the status of your phone.

CHANGE SHOOTING METHOD AND MODE

Set your shooting Method.

Customizing your shooting methods allows you to capture photos and videos in ways that best suit your style and preferences. Once you open the Camera app by swiping up from the bottom of your screen to access the Apps screen, you can easily access the settings to adjust your shooting methods.

Shooting methods

Press Volume buttons to
Take picture or record video

Voice commands
Take pictures by saying "Smile", "Cheese",
"Capture", or "Shoot", or record videos by
saying "Record Video".

Floating Shutter button
Take pictures with an extra Shutter button
you can move anywhere on the screen.

To get started, tap the Quick Controls icon, represented by four dots, and then tap on the Settings icon. From here, select Shooting Methods, which will bring you to a screen where several options are available for personalizing how you take photos and record videos.

One of the options is the Press Volume buttons setting, which allows you to decide how the volume buttons on your device behave during photography. You can choose to use the volume buttons for taking pictures or recording videos, zooming in or out, or adjusting the sound volume. However, it's important to note that if the volume buttons are set to take pictures or record videos, you won't be able to adjust the sound while recording.

Another option is Voice commands, which lets you take photos or start recording videos simply by using preset voice commands. This can be especially useful if you're taking a selfie or need to operate the camera hands-free.

The Floating Shutter button option is also available, which enables a second shutter button that you can position anywhere on the screen.

This gives you more flexibility and control over your shots, especially when holding the phone at difficult angles.

For those who love taking selfies, the Show palm feature allows you to trigger the camera by simply showing your palm to the lens. This makes it easier to capture selfies without needing to press any buttons.

Once you've configured the shooting methods to your liking, tap Back twice to return to the viewfinder, and your new settings will be ready for use. This customization helps streamline the process of capturing images and videos, making it more convenient and tailored to your needs.

Pick a Shooting Mode

Switching between shooting modes is a simple and effective way to enhance your photography and video recording experience. The Camera app offers a variety of modes designed for different scenarios, allowing you to effortlessly capture the best shots depending on the environment or subject. These modes are located at the bottom of the Camera app's screen, and switching between them is as easy as swiping.

When you open the Camera app, you'll see the available shooting modes displayed at the bottom of the screen. By swiping left or right, you can browse through the different options, each tailored to specific photography or video recording needs. Once you find the mode that suits your current situation, simply tap on it to select it. The active mode will be highlighted, making it clear which setting is currently in use.

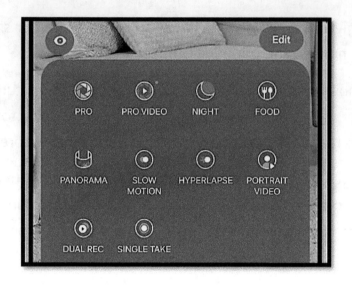

For example, if you're shooting in low-light conditions, you can select Night mode. This mode is specifically designed to help you capture clear photos in dim lighting without the need for a flash, ensuring that your images retain more detail and color.

Other shooting modes available in the Camera app include Portrait, which adds background effects to photos, allowing you to create professional-looking portraits. Photo mode is the standard option for taking regular pictures, where the camera automatically adjusts settings for optimal results. Video mode allows you to record videos, with the camera adjusting the settings to ensure the best video quality.

If you want more options, tap on More to access additional modes. If you find yourself using a specific mode often, you can easily add it to the bottom of the screen for quicker access. To do this, tap on Edit, then drag your preferred mode to the bottom and tap Save.

For those who prefer more control, the Pro and Pro Video modes allow you to manually adjust various settings such as ISO sensitivity, exposure value, white balance, and color tone. These modes are ideal for users who want to fine-tune their shots for more creative or professional results, both in photos and videos.

The Portrait Video mode is similar to Portrait for photos, but it's designed specifically for videos, allowing you to add and adjust background effects while recording. Panorama mode is perfect for capturing wide landscapes, letting you create expansive images by taking photos horizontally or vertically.

If you want to capture multiple perspectives at once, Dual Rec allows you to record a video using both the rear and front cameras simultaneously, giving you a dynamic, split-screen effect. The Food mode is designed to enhance the vivid colors of food, making it a great option for food photography.

When you want to experiment with motion, Slow Motion allows you to record videos at a high frame rate, so you can slow down the footage for dramatic effects. For a more artistic take on time, Hyperlapse lets you create time-lapse videos, adjusting the frame rate based on the scene's movement and the phone's motion.

Each of these modes serves a specific purpose, making your photography and videography more versatile and tailored to different environments or subjects. Whether you're taking a quick selfie, capturing a scenic landscape, or recording a time-lapse video, the shooting modes on the Galaxy S25 provide a range of options to enhance your creative process.

Zoom in and out

The Samsung Galaxy S25 offers incredible zoom capabilities that allow you to capture distant subjects with stunning clarity. When taking a photo or recording a video, the zoom feature lets you get up close to your subject, even if it's far away, ensuring you don't miss a single detail. One of the standout features of this phone is the Space Zoom, which enables up to 100x magnification, making it possible to capture remarkable shots even from several hundred feet away.

To start using the zoom feature, open the Camera app and tap on PHOTO mode. Once you're in photo mode, select the rear camera to begin capturing your shots. You can zoom in by simply pinching the screen with your fingers, which will allow you to focus on distant objects. Alternatively, you can use the zoom controls at the bottom of the screen to zoom in and out.

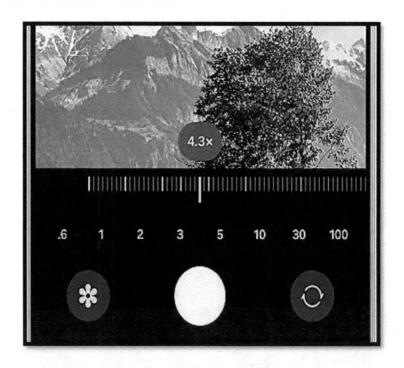

When you zoom in past 10x, the Space Zoom feature is automatically activated. As you zoom further, a small thumbnail of your target will appear in the corner of the screen. This thumbnail acts as a helpful guide, allowing you to better center your shot as you zoom in more and more. This ensures that even at the highest magnification, your photos remain steady and focused.

The Zoom-in mic feature lets you enhance the sound when you're filming. As you zoom in on a subject, the microphone will pick up sounds from that direction with greater intensity, making it ideal for capturing distant conversations or the nuances of far-off scenes. This feature is usually turned on by default, but if you'd like to double-check, you can do so by opening the Camera app, tapping the Quick controls icon (the four dots), then selecting the Settings icon. From there, navigate to Advanced video options, where you'll find the option to enable or disable the Zoom-in mic.

This combination of high-powered zoom and enhanced audio capture makes the Galaxy S25 an excellent tool for both photographers and videographers who want to get closer to their subjects, even from a distance. Whether you're recording a nature documentary, capturing a live event, or taking detailed photos of distant landmarks, the Zoom capabilities and the Zoom-in mic will help you create sharp, clear, and immersive content.

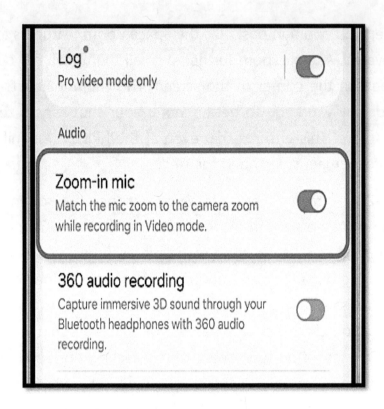

Quick Controls and Tools

The Galaxy S25 series offers a range of helpful camera tools designed to enhance your photography and video experience. These tools make it easy to adjust settings and apply effects, allowing you to achieve the perfect shot or video with minimal effort. All of these tools are accessible through the Quick Controls menu in the Camera app, which you can access by tapping the four-dot icon located within the app. Once you open the Quick controls, a variety of options will be available to assist with your shooting.

One of the most essential tools is the Settings option, which allows you to open the Camera settings menu. From here, you can make adjustments to camera preferences and other advanced features, ensuring your device is set up exactly how you want it for different situations. Another useful tool is the Flash setting, where you can quickly enable or disable the flash, or choose the automatic flash option. This comes in handy when shooting in low-light conditions or when you need to control the amount of light in your photos.

The Timer tool is another valuable feature, allowing you to set a delay before the camera takes a photo or starts recording. This gives you time to get into position, especially when taking selfies or group shots. For those who prefer specific image dimensions, the Ratio tool lets you choose the aspect ratio for your shots, whether you want a standard 4:3 ratio, a widescreen 16:9, or other options.

If you want to control the image quality, the Resolution option lets you choose the resolution of your photos or videos, allowing for higher or lower quality depending on your needs. For added creativity, the Motion photo feature lets you capture a brief video clip right before you press the capture button, giving you the option to add a sense of movement to your still photos. This is great for moments where you want to preserve the action leading up to the shot.

The Exposure tool is perfect for fine-tuning the lighting of your photo or video. You can use the slider to adjust the exposure level, making your images brighter or darker depending on the environment. If you're looking to add a personal touch to your shots, the Filters option lets you apply different filters, or you can download new ones from the Galaxy Store. You can also adjust each filter's strength, color temperature, contrast, saturation, and even film grain to create the desired effect.

Lastly, the Face tool is a great addition for those who take selfies frequently. This tool automatically adjusts the settings to ensure that your face is the focal point of the image, enhancing your features and making sure your selfies look their best. With these camera tools at your disposal, the Galaxy S25 offers a highly customizable photography experience, making it easier to capture stunning images and videos every time.

Access the Camera Setting

The Camera app is packed with intelligent features that allow you to customize your shooting experience to make it more efficient and convenient. To access the Camera settings, open the Camera app and tap the Quick Controls icon (the four dots). From there, tap on the Settings icon to bring up a variety of options that let you tailor the camera's performance to suit your preferences.

Intelligent Feature

One of the standout features in the Camera settings is the Scan documents and text option. This tool automatically detects documents in the frame and displays a button that allows you to scan the document. If you prefer a hands-free experience, you can enable Auto scanning, which allows the camera to automatically scan the document as soon as it detects it, without needing to tap anything. This is particularly useful when you're trying to quickly capture a document or text. The camera can also remove unwanted objects, such as your fingers or other distractions, from the frame to ensure a cleaner scan.

Another useful option is the ability to Scan QR codes automatically. When enabled, your camera will detect QR codes in the frame without the need to manually focus on them, making it quicker and easier to scan codes when you're out and about.

The Shot suggestions feature provides helpful on-screen guides that assist you in aligning your shots for better composition. This is especially beneficial for users who are still learning the ropes of photography or for anyone who wants to ensure their photos are framed properly every time. The camera will provide visual cues that guide you toward capturing balanced, well-composed images.

For those who like to adjust the camera's performance based on different needs, the Intelligent optimization setting allows you to prioritize either quality or speed in Photo mode. If you prefer faster shutter speeds for capturing action shots, you can prioritize speed, whereas if you want the highest quality images possible, you can opt to prioritize quality. Additionally, enabling the Scene optimizer enhances the camera's ability to automatically adjust important elements like exposure, contrast, and white balance depending on what the camera detects in the scene. This feature works particularly well with the rear camera, adjusting settings to optimize your photos based on the lighting and subject in front of you.

These intelligent features are designed to make your photography experience more seamless, efficient, and enjoyable. By customizing these settings, you can have the right tools at your fingertips to capture photos and documents with ease and ensure your shots are always optimized for the best results.

Taking Pictures

The Camera app provides several advanced features designed to give you more control over how you take and save photos, allowing you to personalize your photography experience further. One of these features is the Swipe Shutter button option, which offers a more dynamic way to capture images. By swiping the shutter button to the edge of the screen, you can choose to take a burst shot, capturing a series of fast-paced images in quick succession, or create a GIF, which is a fun and engaging way to capture a sequence of images and turn them into an animated file. This feature is great for capturing movement or moments that unfold quickly, providing you with more creative ways to document your experiences.

Another option that allows you to add a unique touch to your photos is the Watermark feature. This option lets you place a watermark on your photos, which is especially useful for branding your images or adding personalized information. You can customize the watermark to include details such as the date, time, location, or even your custom text. This feature not only helps protect your photos but also adds a professional touch to your work, making it easy to showcase where and when your photos were taken.

For users who want to have more control over how their photos are saved, the Advanced picture options offer a variety of settings to choose from. These options allow you to decide on things like the image format, the resolution of the photo, and how your photos are stored, helping you manage storage space while still getting the best quality possible. Whether you prefer to save images in a particular format for easier sharing or to maintain high resolution for printing, these advanced settings ensure that your photos are saved exactly how you want them.

Together, these features make the Samsung Galaxy S25 Camera app more versatile, offering creative and practical tools for enhancing your photography while allowing for customization to suit your specific needs.

Exploring Selfies

The Samsung Galaxy S25 offers convenient features to enhance your selfie-taking experience, making it easier to capture the perfect shot exactly how you want it. One such feature is the option to save selfies as previewed, which allows you to keep your selfies as they appear on the screen during the preview, without flipping them. This means that what you see in the preview, including any angles or orientations, is exactly what will be saved, helping you avoid any surprises when you review your photo afterward. It provides more flexibility and accuracy for those who prefer their selfies to be captured in their natural state, without any automatic mirroring or adjustments.

The swipe up/down to switch cameras feature makes it easy to toggle between the front and rear cameras. By simply swiping up or down on the screen, you can quickly switch from taking selfies to capturing photos with the rear camera, without having to press multiple buttons or navigate through menus. This swipe gesture is intuitive and efficient, streamlining the process of switching cameras so you can quickly capture any moment, whether you're in the frame or focusing on something else.

These features are designed to make the process of taking and saving selfies on the Galaxy S25 smoother, more customizable, and intuitive, ensuring you always get the shot just the way you want.

Taking Videos

The variety of video features is designed to enhance your recording experience when capturing moments in bright sunlight or low-light settings. One such feature is Auto FPS, which automatically adjusts the frame rate to optimize video brightness when shooting in darker conditions. This feature ensures that your videos remain clear and well-lit, even when the surrounding light is insufficient. Optimizing the frame rate, allows you to capture smoother, brighter videos without the need for manual adjustments, making it easier to record high-quality footage regardless of the lighting situation.

Another important video feature is video stabilization, which helps reduce camera shake and ensures that your videos remain steady even when the camera is moving. This is especially useful when recording in dynamic environments, such as when walking or moving. The anti-shake feature smooths out the footage, keeping the focus sharp and minimizing blurriness, which is crucial for creating professional-looking videos, even when you're on the go.

For those who want even more control over their video recordings, the Advanced video options provide a variety of settings to improve the quality and versatility of your footage. These options include High-efficiency videos, which allow you to record videos in a more compressed format without sacrificing quality, saving storage space while still maintaining a high level of detail. High-bitrate videos provide a richer, more detailed video experience, ideal for those who want the highest quality available. Additionally, HDR videos offer better contrast and colors, making your videos appear more vibrant, especially in high-contrast environments with both bright and dark areas.

The Zoom-in mic feature allows you to focus on specific sounds as you zoom in while recording, making it ideal for capturing distant conversations or sounds in more detail. Another notable feature is 360 audio recording, which captures sound from all directions, creating a more immersive and realistic audio experience that complements 360-degree video recording. Lastly, Audio playback enhances the sound quality of videos during playback, ensuring that the audio is clear and balanced when watching your recordings later.

These video features give you the flexibility to capture high-quality footage in any situation, from dynamic outdoor scenes to quiet indoor environments. Whether you're a professional videographer or just someone who enjoys documenting everyday moments, the Galaxy S25's video capabilities provide a range of tools to make your recordings as smooth, detailed, and immersive as possible.

General

The camera offers a variety of settings to enhance the photography and video recording experience. One of the key features is Tracking autofocus, which helps you keep a moving subject in focus. This is especially useful when filming action scenes or capturing fast-moving objects, ensuring that the subject remains sharp even if it shifts position. This feature allows you to take clearer and more dynamic photos and videos without worrying about losing focus as things move.

Another helpful tool is the Composition guide, which provides a visual aid for framing your shots. By displaying level and viewfinder grid lines, the guide helps you line up your photos and videos for better composition. Whether you're aiming for symmetry, using the rule of thirds, or simply making sure everything is aligned, this feature ensures that your shots are more visually appealing and balanced.

To make your photos more connected, you can use Location tags, which attach a GPS tag to your pictures and videos. This is useful for keeping track of where you captured certain images or for sharing your location with others. Whether you're traveling or just documenting your daily activities, location tags provide an added layer of context to your media.

When it comes to shooting methods, the camera offers several options that can be customized to fit your preferences. You can use the Press Volume buttons to feature to take photos or videos, control zoom, or adjust the sound volume, providing versatility at your fingertips. Voice commands allow you to snap photos or start recording videos with simple spoken commands, offering hands-free convenience. If you prefer more control, the Floating Shutter button lets you place an additional shutter button anywhere on the screen, making it easier to take photos from various angles. The Show Palm feature enables you to take selfies by simply showing the palm of your hand to the camera, simplifying the process of snapping the perfect selfie without needing to press the shutter.

For those who like to keep their shooting process consistent, the Settings to Keep feature allows you to save your previous shooting settings, such as the mode, selfie angle, and applied filters. This way, you can continue where you left off without having to reconfigure your preferences every time you open the camera app.

To add another layer of customization, you can choose to enable or disable the Shutter sound. This feature plays a tone when taking a picture, providing an audible confirmation that your photo has been captured. Additionally, if you prefer tactile feedback, the Vibration feedback setting lets you feel a vibration when you tap the screen in the Camera app, giving you a more sensory way of interacting with the camera.

These settings work together to create a flexible and intuitive photography experience, allowing you to capture photos and videos with ease and precision while offering multiple ways to personalize your camera's functionality. Whether you're shooting stills, videos, or selfies, the Galaxy S25 provides the tools needed to bring your creative vision to life.

Use Bixby Vision

Bixby Vision is an intelligent feature that enhances your experience by providing useful information about your surroundings. Integrated directly into the Camera app, Bixby Vision allows you to scan objects, text, and scenes, offering insights and actions based on what it detects. This feature brings a whole new level of interaction, helping you learn more about the world around you.

To use Bixby Vision, open the Camera app and tap on MORE to access additional options. From there, tap the Bixby Vision icon, represented by an eye. If prompted, grant the necessary permissions to allow the app to access the camera and other features. Once Bixby Vision is activated, you will be presented with a variety of options, each designed to assist with different tasks.

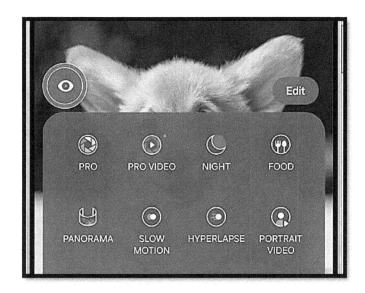

For instance, the Translate feature allows you to point the camera at any text, and Bixby Vision will automatically translate it into the language of your choice. You can select the language you prefer from the top of the screen, making it incredibly useful for reading signs, menus, or documents in a foreign language.

If you're dealing with printed text, the Text option lets you capture a selection of text simply by pointing the camera at it. After Bixby Vision scans the text, you can choose to copy, translate, or share it, saving you time and effort when handling written content.

For discovering new things, the Discover feature allows you to point your camera at an object, and Bixby Vision will search for similar items on Pinterest. This is a fun way to explore similar products, designs, or ideas that match what you've scanned.

If you're interested in wine, the Wine feature lets you scan a wine bottle, and Bixby Vision will provide you with details like the bottle's rating and additional information about the vineyard it came from, helping you make informed decisions when picking out wine.

For those who need assistance with their environment, the Scene Describer feature is incredibly helpful. When you point the camera at something, Bixby Vision will provide an audio description of the scene, helping you understand what is in front of you. Similarly, the Object Identifier feature will describe any object or item you scan, giving you valuable information about what you're looking at, especially useful for unfamiliar objects.

The Text Reader function goes a step further by reading aloud any text you scan, helping users who may have difficulty reading small print or who prefer an auditory experience. Lastly, the Color Detector feature lets you point the camera at something, and it will audibly tell you what color it is, providing additional assistance for those who are visually impaired or anyone curious about color identification.

Bixby Vision is a powerful tool that opens up a wide range of possibilities, from translating languages to identifying objects, all from the convenience of your phone's camera. Whether you're traveling, shopping, or just exploring, this feature helps you engage with the world around you in a more informed and interactive way.

Use Galaxy Avatar

The Galaxy S25 offers an exciting feature called Galaxy Avatar, which allows you to create a personalized digital representation of yourself that you can use in photos. This feature allows you to customize an avatar, which can be a fun way to express yourself and even take creative, personalized photos.

To get started with your Galaxy Avatar, first, open the Settings app on your device. From there, navigate to Advanced Features, and then select Galaxy Avatar. This will open the options where you can create and customize your avatar.

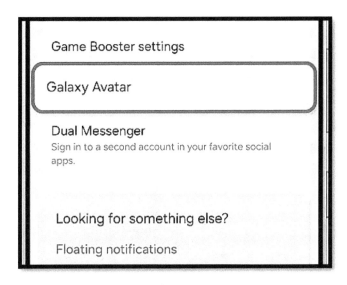

Next, tap on Avatar Camera to begin the process. When prompted, tap the screen to start creating your avatar. You have the option to either use the Camera app to create your avatar or use an existing image from your Gallery app. If you don't want to create an avatar from scratch, you can also choose from a selection of premade avatars available at the top of the screen.

The setup process will ask for certain permissions, which you'll need to allow to proceed. Follow the on-screen instructions to fine-tune the appearance of your avatar. Once your avatar is ready, you can start using it to take fun and unique photos. At the bottom of the screen, you'll find options to adjust your photo style, such as Scene, Mask, Mirror, or Play, which let you customize how the avatar interacts with your environment in the photo.

If you want to make adjustments to your avatar after you've created it, tap the Edit avatar icon, represented by a person. This allows you to change different features of your avatar, ensuring it accurately represents you or suits your desired style.

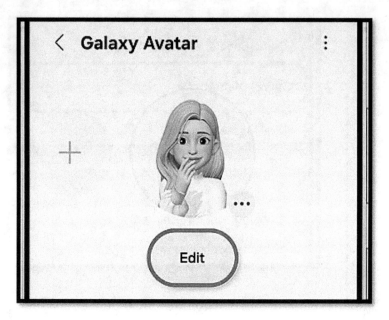

To enhance your photo further, you can change the background color by tapping the Change background icon, which is represented by a paint can. This feature allows you to customize the backdrop of your avatar photo, making it even more personal and dynamic.

After capturing your photo, you can view it immediately by tapping the Gallery thumbnail or by opening the Gallery app directly. Your personalized avatar photo is now saved and ready for sharing or personal use, offering a fun way to express yourself through a digital version of yourself.

This Galaxy Avatar feature provides a new, interactive way to create and enjoy personalized media, allowing for greater creativity and customization in your photos. Whether you're using it for fun, social media, or simply as a cool way to represent yourself, your Galaxy S25 ensures a unique and personalized experience every time.

Camera Share

The Camera Share feature allows you to transform your phone into a portable webcam, making it a convenient tool for video calls no matter where you are. This feature is especially useful if you don't have access to a traditional webcam or want to use the high-quality camera on your Galaxy S25 for better video call performance.

To enable Camera Share, start by opening the Settings app on your phone. From there, navigate to Connected Devices, and then tap on Camera Share. At the top of the screen, you'll see a switch to turn the feature on. Once activated, your Galaxy S25 will be ready to be used as a webcam for video calls.

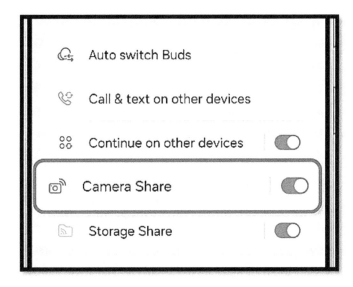

After enabling Camera Share, you can start a video call using your preferred apps, such as Google Meet, Zoom, or any other video conferencing platform that supports webcam functionality. The camera on your phone will now act as the video feed, giving you the flexibility to participate in video calls with the added benefit of using your phone's high-resolution camera.

This feature is particularly helpful when you need to join a video call in a pinch, allowing you to use your phone's superior camera quality for clearer, sharper video without needing additional equipment. Whether you're working remotely, catching up with friends, or attending virtual meetings, Camera Share makes it easier to stay connected with others.

Capturing High-Quality Photos and Videos

To begin capturing high-resolution photos, open the Camera app by tapping the camera icon on your home screen. Once the camera app is launched, you will need to adjust the aspect ratio to ensure you're using the highest resolution available for your shots. Tap on the Camera Ratio option within the app to bring up the settings where you can choose different aspect ratios for your photos.

For the highest resolution, select the 3:4 (64MP High Resolution) option. This setting allows you to take photos at an impressive 64MP, ensuring that every detail in your shot is captured with maximum clarity. The higher the resolution, the more detailed and sharper your images will be, especially when zooming in on specific areas or when you want to print your photos at larger sizes without losing quality.

Once you've selected the desired ratio and are satisfied with the settings, you can go ahead and take your high-resolution shot. Simply tap the Shutter button, and the camera will capture the image in the selected 64MP resolution. With this high-quality setting, your photos will show off the vivid colors and intricate details that make your images stand out. This feature is perfect for those who want to capture professional-grade photos with their phone, whether for personal use or more serious photography projects.

EDITING PHOTOS WITH BUILT-IN TOOLS

Using Generative Edit

Generative editing offers a powerful way to transform your photos by allowing you to move or remove objects, creating a completely new image. This feature uses Galaxy AI to automatically fill in the background and any missing portions, giving you the flexibility to manipulate your photos with ease. Whether you're adjusting an image to enhance its composition or creatively removing elements, generative editing provides the tools to do so seamlessly.

To get started, open the Gallery app and select the photo you'd like to edit. Once you've opened the image, tap the Edit icon (represented by a pencil), and then tap the Generative edit icon (the blue circle with three stars). You may be prompted to tap OK to confirm that you want to use this feature.

Using your finger, outline the object you wish to move or remove. If you make a mistake or want to try again, simply tap Deselect to start over and adjust your selection. After selecting the object, you can touch and hold it to drag it to a different part of the image. If you decide you want the object back in its original position, just tap Return (the back arrow). Alternatively, if you want to remove the object from the image entirely, tap the Remove option, which is represented by an eraser icon. You can repeat this process to move or delete as many objects as needed.

If the photo needs further adjustments, you can use the slider at the bottom of the screen to straighten the image, ensuring that everything aligns perfectly. Once you're satisfied with the changes, tap Generate. Galaxy AI will then automatically fill in the background and make any necessary adjustments to the image, ensuring that the picture looks natural and complete, despite the changes you've made.

After generating the new image, you can compare it to the original by holding down the View original button. This allows you to see a side-by-side comparison, ensuring you're happy with the changes. Once you're done editing and satisfied with the result, tap Done, then select Save as copy to save the newly generated image, leaving the original untouched. With generative editing, you can easily manipulate your photos and create unique, professional-looking images with minimal effort.

Use Edit Suggestion

The Edit suggestions feature leverages the power of Galaxy AI to automatically analyze your photos and offer tailored recommendations to improve their quality. These suggestions are designed to enhance various aspects of your images, depending on what Galaxy AI detects, such as blurring the background for more focus or even remastering the photo to sharpen its clarity. The suggestions may vary from one image to another, and in some cases, there may not be any suggestions provided at all. However, when available, these AI-powered enhancements can significantly elevate your photos with minimal effort on your part.

To start using the Edit suggestions, open the Gallery app on your device and select the image you want to improve. Once the photo is displayed, tap the Details icon (the i symbol) or the AI icon (the three stars), which will reveal the available editing suggestions that Galaxy AI has identified for your image. These suggestions might include options like Remaster, which enhances the overall quality of your photo by improving its sharpness, contrast, or colors, or Erase shadows, which can help eliminate unwanted shadows from the image to give it a cleaner look. Another option could be Erase reflections, which can remove any reflections that are distracting or unwanted in your photo.

After selecting your preferred suggestion, follow the on-screen instructions to apply the changes. You may need to tap or draw around specific objects within the image to refine the edit or adjust a slider bar to fine-tune the effect. The process is intuitive and gives you control over how the final result will appear. Whether you want to improve the brightness, and contrast, or even remove specific elements, the Edit Suggestions feature allows you to easily optimize your photos without requiring advanced editing skills.

By using Galaxy AI's intelligent suggestions, you can quickly enhance your images, ensuring they look their best with minimal time and effort. When making small adjustments or completely transforming your photos, this feature provides a simple and effective way to take your images to the next level.

Use AI Drawing and Sketch to image

The AI Drawing and Sketch to Image feature offers a way to enhance your photos by adding AI-generated drawings directly onto them. This feature allows you to sketch and draw on images, and then use Galaxy AI to turn your sketches into refined, professional-looking drawings, all with just your finger or an S Pen. It's a perfect tool for anyone looking to add a personalized touch to their photos, whether you're creating artwork or simply having fun.

To get started, open the Gallery app and select the photo you want to work with. Once you've chosen the image, tap the Photo Assist icon, which is represented by stars, and then select the Sketch to Image option. This will open the drawing interface, allowing you to start adding your sketches to the image. Using your finger or S Pen, you can begin drawing directly on the image, whether you're sketching an object, adding details, or creating an entirely new element.

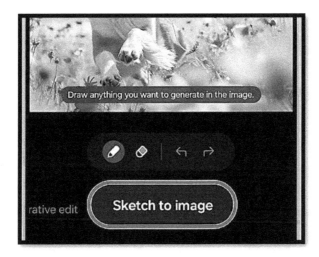

If you make any mistakes or wish to adjust your drawing, you can easily undo or redo your actions using the arrows provided in the app. For more precise adjustments, the eraser tool lets you remove any parts of the drawing you no longer want. This flexibility makes it easy to experiment and refine your creations until you're satisfied with the result.

Once you've finished your sketch, tap Generate, and Galaxy AI will process your drawing and enhance it to create a polished, AI-generated image based on your sketch. You can then swipe through the generated versions until you find one that matches your vision. Whether you want a more artistic look or something closer to the original, the AI will adapt to the style of your drawing.

When you're happy with the final result, tap **Save Copy** to preserve your newly enhanced image. This allows you to keep your original photo while saving the AI-enhanced version with your custom sketch, ready to be shared or used however you see fit.

This AI-powered feature provides a seamless way to add a creative twist to your photos. Whether you're an artist, a designer, or someone who just enjoys customizing their images, the Sketch to Image feature on the Galaxy Z Flip6 gives you the freedom to create and enhance photos with ease.

Use Portrait Studio

Once you've captured a selfie, you can enhance it further by using Portrait Studio to add artistic flair and transform your photo into something unique. Go to the Gallery app and select the selfie you want to edit. Once you've chosen your image, tap the Photo Assist icon, represented by stars, and then select the Generative Portrait option to begin customizing your selfie.

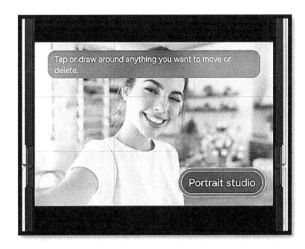

Portrait Studio offers several creative styles that allow you to reimagine your selfie with a professional touch. You'll see various options at the bottom of the screen, including styles like Comic, 3D Cartoon, or Watercolor. Each style provides a different artistic effect, from the playful and colorful feel of a comic-style rendering to the elegant and soft look of watercolor. After selecting the style that best suits your mood or the image you want to create, tap Generate to let the AI process the transformation.

Once the AI has generated several versions of your selfie in the chosen style, you can swipe through the options to view all the variations. This gives you the flexibility to compare and select the image that best matches your vision. Whether you prefer a bold, cartoonish look or a soft, artistic watercolor feel, you can easily find a result that enhances your original photo.

When you've found the version you like, simply tap Save Copy to preserve the newly created image. This allows you to keep both your original selfie and the edited, stylized version, which you can then share with friends, use on social media, or save for future reference. With Portrait Studio, you can add a touch of creativity and professional artistry to your selfies, turning simple snapshots into stunning pieces of art with ease.

Use Live Effect

The Live Effect feature adds an exciting dimension to your photos by animating them. This effect brings motion to your images, enhancing them with dynamic movements that vary based on the content of the photo.

Go to the Gallery app and select the photo you'd like to animate. After selecting your image, swipe up to access additional details, then tap on the 3D photo. The AI will process the image and apply an animation effect, which could include actions like zooming, panning, or swiveling, depending on what the photo contains. These effects add an engaging, lifelike quality to your photos.

Once the animation is applied, you can share it with others by tapping the Share button at the bottom of the screen, making it easy to send to friends or post on social media. If you'd prefer to keep the animated version for yourself, you can tap Save Copy to store it on your device.

With Live Effect, you can turn static images into interactive, visually captivating content, giving a fresh and dynamic feel to your photos.

Use Galaxy Enhance-X

The Galaxy Enhance-X app, available for download in the Galaxy Store, is an excellent tool for taking your photos to the next level. This app is designed to help you refine and improve your images, offering a range of powerful editing features that allow you to enhance your pictures with just a few taps. If you want to brighten up a dull photo, sharpen the focus, or increase the resolution for better clarity, this app gives you the ability to do so with ease.

One of the standout features of Galaxy Enhance-X is its ability to brighten photos, making them appear more vibrant and well-lit, even in challenging lighting conditions. If you have an image that looks a bit blurry or lacks sharpness, the Sharpen tool helps to bring the details back into focus, ensuring that your images are crisp and clear. Additionally, the Restore Picture option allows you to repair damaged or low-quality images, bringing back lost details and improving the overall appearance of old or degraded photos.

For those who want to capture more intricate details, the Increase Resolution feature provides a way to enhance the resolution of your images, making them look more defined and suitable for larger prints or detailed views. These tools, along with other editing options available in the app, ensure that you can customize your photos to match your vision and achieve professional-quality results directly from your phone.

With Galaxy Enhance-X, you gain the flexibility and control to elevate the quality of your photos, whether you're enhancing a simple snapshot or fine-tuning an image for sharing or printing. This app is a great companion for anyone who loves photography and wants to make their images look their best with minimal effort.

Use Audio eraser

The Audio Eraser feature is an incredibly useful tool that allows you to remove unwanted background noise from your videos, leaving only the essential sounds you want to capture. This feature makes it easier to focus on the main audio in your videos, such as speech or music, by eliminating distractions like traffic noise, wind, or other environmental sounds.

To get started, open the Gallery app and select the video you want to edit. Once the video is open, tap the Edit icon, represented by a pencil, to access the editing options. From the editing menu, tap the Audio icon, which looks like a speaker, located in the bottom right corner of the screen. You will then see the Audio Eraser option, which you should tap to begin the process of removing unwanted audio.

Once the feature is activated, you can preview your video by tapping the Play icon to listen to the playback with the audio adjustments applied. If you want to hear the original audio before the changes, you can tap Hear the original at the top of the screen. This allows you to compare the edited version with the original one to ensure the changes meet your expectations. Alternatively, if you prefer to mute all the sounds in the video, you can tap the Mute button at the bottom of the screen, which will silence all audio in the video entirely.

This Audio Eraser tool provides a simple and efficient way to enhance your videos by giving you control over the sound. Whether you're cleaning up a noisy recording or enhancing the audio for a more professional result, the Galaxy S25's Audio Eraser feature helps ensure your videos sound clear and focused, free from unnecessary distractions.

CHAPTER 7

CONNECTIVITY AND SHARING

Sharing Files with Nearby Share and Quick Share

Quick Share

To start using the Quick Share feature and transfer files between devices, the first step is to ensure that Quick Share is enabled on both devices. On the second device you're sharing with, open the notification panel by swiping down from the top of the screen. Look for the Quick Share icon, and tap on it to turn it on. The icon will turn blue when the feature is active. If you don't see the Quick Share icon in your Quick Settings, it's possible that it hasn't been added. In that case, you will need to go into the Quick Settings menu and manually add the icon for easier access.

Next, open the Gallery app on your phone and select the image you want to share. After selecting the image, tap the Share button, and a list of nearby devices will appear. Choose the device you want to send the image to and confirm the transfer request on the other device. Once the file transfer is accepted, the image will begin to transfer wirelessly.

If you're experiencing difficulties connecting to the other device, you can try adjusting the Quick Share settings. Open the Quick Settings by swiping down from the top of your screen, then press and hold the Quick Share icon. In the settings menu that appears, you'll see an option to Show my position to others. Enabling this setting will allow your device to be visible to nearby devices when they are using Quick

Share. This feature is helpful when you're not able to find your device on the other person's list, as it ensures your device is discoverable. Please note that the Show My Position to Others option is available only on certain device models.

To further optimize the sharing process, ensure that your phone's visibility is turned on. If your device is not visible, you may need to head into the Settings app, go to Connections, and toggle the Phone Visibility option to On. This ensures that your device will appear on nearby devices when sharing files. Another important tip is that you can share files with up to five devices at once, making it very convenient for sending content to multiple people simultaneously.

Remember, the other person's screen must be on to receive the file, and sharing over a mobile network may incur additional charges. The Quick Share feature requires the receiving device to support Wi-Fi Direct, and Wi-Fi must be enabled on both devices for the transfer to work. While transferring, keep in mind that the maximum size for a single file transfer is 1GB, and you can send up to 2GB of data per day.

The Quick Share feature is compatible with devices running Android Q OS and later, though the availability of targets and devices that can receive files may differ depending on the model. This tool offers a fast and easy way to send images, documents, or other files between compatible devices without the hassle of cables or complex setups. Whether you're sending files to friends, colleagues, or family, Quick Share makes sharing content effortless and efficient.

Nearby Share

Nearby Share is a feature that enables you to share files, photos, and links with nearby devices seamlessly. To use Nearby Share, ensure that both devices have Bluetooth, Wi-Fi, and Location services turned on. When someone sends you a file, you'll receive a notification prompting you to accept or decline the transfer. Additionally, you can set an expiration date for shared files, ensuring they remain accessible only for a specified period. This feature is particularly useful for quickly sharing content without the need for internet connectivity or physical connections.

Connecting to External Devices (Smart TVs, Laptops)

Setting up Samsung DeX wirelessly and connecting it to your Samsung Smart Monitor, begin by ensuring that both devices are powered on. On your Smart Monitor, use the remote control or the physical buttons to navigate to the Source menu and select Screen Mirroring. This action prepares the monitor to receive a wireless connection.

On your Galaxy S25, access the Quick Settings panel by swiping down from the top of the screen. Tap the DeX icon to open the DeX menu. Within this menu, choose the option labeled DeX on TV or Monitor. Your device will then search for available displays. Once your Smart Monitor appears in the list, tap on it to initiate the connection.

After a brief moment, the DeX interface will appear on your Smart Monitor, providing a desktop-like experience. For navigation, you can use your Galaxy S25 as a touchpad. To enable this, tap the Touchpad icon on your device's screen. This allows you to control the cursor on the monitor by swiping on your phone's display.

For a more traditional desktop experience, consider connecting a Bluetooth keyboard and mouse to your Galaxy S25. This setup enhances productivity by providing familiar input methods, making it easier to interact with applications and manage tasks on the larger screen.

By following these steps, you can seamlessly extend your Galaxy S25's functionality to your Samsung Smart Monitor, creating a versatile workspace that combines the portability of your smartphone with the expansive display of your monitor.

Adding a keyboard and mouse

Enhancing your Samsung DeX experience by connecting a Bluetooth keyboard and mouse can provide a more traditional desktop-like environment. Begin by ensuring that both your keyboard and mouse are in pairing mode, following the manufacturer's instructions. On your Galaxy S25, open the Settings app and navigate to the Bluetooth menu. Here, you should see a list of available devices. Select your keyboard and mouse from this list to initiate the pairing process. You may be prompted to enter a verification code on your keyboard to complete the pairing.

Once paired, you can use your DeX-enabled device to work in your favorite productivity apps, including Google Workspace, Cisco Webex, Microsoft Office, Microsoft Remote Desktop, Citrix Workspace, Zoom Cloud Meetings, and more. This setup allows for efficient navigation and interaction within the DeX environment, making tasks such as document editing, web browsing, and video conferencing more seamless.

MANAGING MOBILE DATA AND HOTSPOTS

Manage Hotspot Settings

First Go to the Settings app. Navigate to Connections.

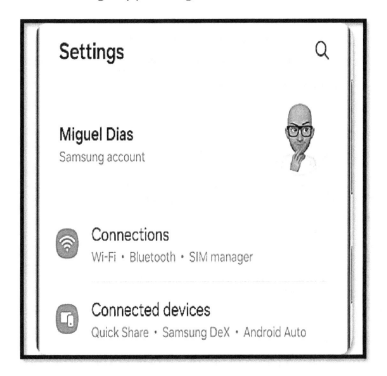

Then select Mobile Hotspot and Tethering, and tap on Mobile Hotspot. Here, you can modify various settings to personalize your hotspot experience.

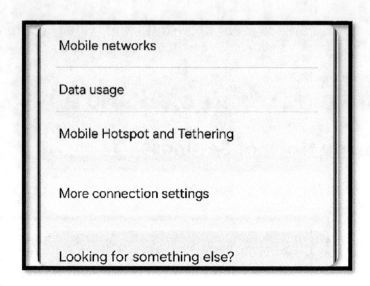

Mobile networks

Data usage

Mobile Hotspot and Tethering

More connection settings

Looking for something else?

To change the network name (SSID), security type, or password, tap on Configure. In this section, you can set a new network name, choose a security type such as WPA2-Personal, and enter a new password. Remember, the new password must be entered on the connecting device to establish a secure connection.

If you wish to remove the existing password, tap the Password field, delete the current password, and leave it blank. After making your desired changes, tap Save to apply them.

For optimal performance, you can select the preferred band for your hotspot. Tap on Band and choose between 2.4 GHz or 5 GHz, depending on your needs. The 5 GHz band typically offers faster speeds but may have a shorter range compared to 2.4 GHz.

To manage the timeout settings for your hotspot, tap on Advanced, then select Turn off when no device is connected. Here, you can choose the duration after which the hotspot will automatically turn off when no devices are connected. Options may include settings like

Never timeout, 5 minutes, 10 minutes, or 60 minutes. After selecting your preferred timeout duration, tap Save to confirm the changes.

By customizing these settings, you can tailor your mobile hotspot to better suit your connectivity needs and preferences.

Manage Data Usage

Start by opening the Settings app. Navigate to Connections,

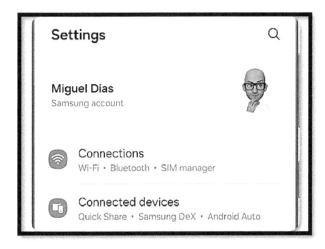

Then select Data Usage. Here, you can monitor your data consumption and adjust settings to help prevent overage charges.

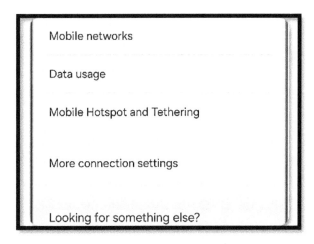

To activate Data Saver, which restricts background data usage by apps, tap on Data Saver and toggle it on. This feature is particularly useful for conserving data when you have a limited plan.

If you wish to set a Mobile Data Limit to automatically disable data once a certain threshold is reached, tap on Billing cycle and data warning. Enable Limit mobile data usage, then set your desired data limit. This ensures that your device will turn off mobile data once the specified limit is exceeded, helping you avoid unexpected charges.

To receive a Mobile Data Warning when approaching a specific data usage level, tap on Set data warning within the same menu. Enable this option and set your preferred warning level. This feature alerts you when your data usage nears the set threshold, allowing you to manage your consumption more effectively.

To adjust your Data Usage Cycle to align with your billing cycle, tap on Start billing cycle. Set the date that matches the first day of your billing cycle, then tap Set. This customization helps you track your data usage by your billing period, providing a clearer overview of your consumption patterns.

By configuring these settings, you can effectively monitor and control your mobile data usage, ensuring that you stay within your plan's limits and avoid additional charges.

Connect to a Wi-Fi Network

For a proper way to Connect to a Wi-Fi network, you will need to access the Settings app on your device. Within the Settings menu, locate and select Connections.

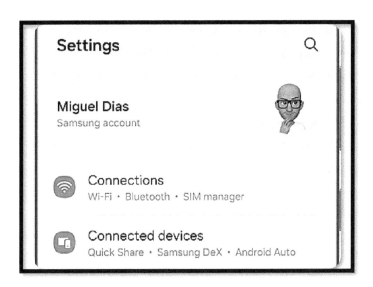

Then tap on **Wi-Fi**. If Wi-Fi is not already enabled, activate it by toggling the switch to the **On** position. This action will prompt your device to search for available networks in your vicinity.

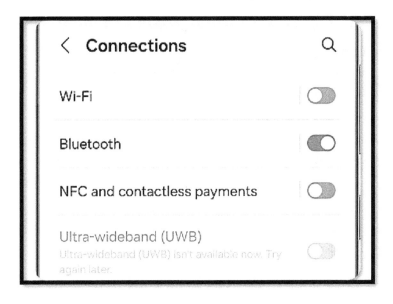

Once the list of available networks appears, identify and select the Wi-Fi network you wish to join.

If the network is secured, a prompt will appear requesting the network password. Enter the correct password and tap **Connect** to establish the connection.

After a successful connection, the network name will be displayed under the Current network section, accompanied by a Connected status indicator. This confirms that your Galaxy S25 is now connected to the selected Wi-Fi network, allowing you to access the internet and other network resources.

CHAPTER 8

TROUBLESHOOTING COMMON ISSUES

Battery and Charging Problems

If your Samsung Galaxy S25 is experiencing charging issues, it's essential to systematically troubleshoot to identify and resolve the problem. Begin by inspecting your charging equipment. Ensure that the charging cable and adapter are in good condition, free from any visible damage such as fraying or exposed wires. If you notice any defects, discontinue use immediately to prevent potential harm to your device.

Next, examine the charging port on your Galaxy S25. Accumulation of dust, lint, or other debris can obstruct the connection between the charging cable and the device, leading to charging problems. Gently inspect the port and, if necessary, use a soft brush or compressed air to clear any obstructions.

After ensuring that both the charging equipment and port are clean and undamaged, reconnect the charging cable to your device and plug it into a power source. Observe the charging indicator on your phone to determine if the issue persists.

If the problem continues, consider testing with an alternative charging cable and adapter to rule out the possibility of faulty equipment. Additionally, try charging your device using a different power outlet to eliminate the outlet as a potential source of the issue.

In some cases, software glitches can interfere with the charging process. Performing a soft reset by restarting your device can help resolve such issues. To do this, press and hold the power button until the restart option appears, then follow the on-screen instructions.

If, after these steps, your Galaxy S25 still fails to charge properly, it may be necessary to consult with a professional technician. Contact Samsung's customer support or visit an authorized service center for further assistance. They can provide a thorough diagnosis and recommend appropriate solutions to restore your device's charging functionality.

By methodically following these troubleshooting steps, you can effectively address and resolve charging issues with your Samsung Galaxy S25, ensuring your device remains operational and reliable.

Fixing Network and Connectivity Issues

Experiencing connectivity issues can be frustrating. To address these problems, it's essential to systematically check and adjust your device's settings.

Begin by verifying your subscription to a 5G plan. Even with a 5G-capable device, lacking a 5G plan can prevent you from accessing 5G networks. Additionally, ensure you're in an area that supports 5G connectivity, as coverage can vary by location.

Next, review your mobile network settings. Navigate to Settings, then Connections, and select Mobile Networks. Here, you can adjust your network mode to prioritize 5G, 4G, or 3G, depending on your needs and network availability.

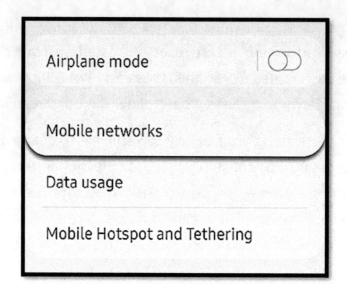

If issues persist, consider resetting your network settings. This action will remove all Bluetooth pairings and stored Wi-Fi networks, so ensure you have the necessary information to reconnect. To proceed, go to Settings, then General Management, tap Reset, and select Reset network settings. Confirm the action by tapping Reset settings and entering your PIN or password if prompted. After resetting, test your mobile connection to see if the problem is resolved.

If connectivity issues continue, it's advisable to contact your carrier for assistance. They can check for any service outages in your area or account-related problems that might be affecting your connection.

Resetting and Restoring Your Device

Factory Data Reset

Performing a factory data reset can be an effective solution for resolving persistent issues or preparing the device for a new user. This process will erase all personal data, settings, and apps, restoring the device to its original factory state.

Before Proceeding:

It's crucial to back up all important data, such as contacts, photos, and documents, to prevent any loss. Ensure your device has sufficient battery life or connect it to a power source to avoid interruptions during the reset process.

Factory Data Reset via Settings:

1. Open the Settings app.

2. Navigate to General management.

3. Tap on Reset, then select Factory data reset.

4. Review the information provided, which outlines the data that will be erased.

5. Tap Reset, and if prompted, enter your device's PIN, password, or pattern.

6. Confirm by tapping Delete All.

7. The device will restart and initiate the reset process, which may take several minutes.

8. Once completed, the device will reboot to the initial setup screen.

Alternative Method: Factory Data Reset via Recovery Mode (If Device is Unresponsive):

If your Galaxy S25 is unresponsive or unable to power on, you can perform a factory reset using the hardware keys:

1. Ensure the device is powered off completely.

2. Press and hold the Volume Up button and the Power button simultaneously.

3. Release both buttons when the Samsung logo appears.

4. Use the volume buttons to navigate to Wipe data/factory reset and press the Power button to select.

5. Confirm the action by selecting Yes.

6. Once the reset is complete, select Reboot system now.

7. The device will restart and may take longer than usual to boot up.

Please note that performing a factory reset will erase all data on your device. Ensure you have backed up all necessary information before proceeding. Additionally, if you have a Samsung account linked to your device, you may need to enter your account credentials after the reset to access certain features.

CHAPTER 9

MAINTENANCE AND DEVICE CARE

Optimizing Device Performance

Experiencing performance slowdowns on your Samsung Galaxy S25 can be attributed to several factors. One common cause is the accumulation of unnecessary files and fragmented storage, which can hinder system performance, causing apps to load slower and the device to become less responsive.

Another factor is the presence of certain applications, especially those running in the background, which can consume significant system resources, decreasing device responsiveness.

Battery degradation over time can lead to reduced performance and shorter battery life.

Thermal throttling, where the device automatically reduces processor speed during intensive tasks or in high-temperature environments to prevent overheating, can also result in perceived slowdowns. Furthermore, software updates can sometimes lead to performance issues, especially if the device is older or if the update is not optimized for the hardware. To address these issues, it's advisable to regularly clear unnecessary files, manage background applications, monitor battery health, ensure proper ventilation during intensive tasks, and keep your device's software updated.

If you're looking to keep your Samsung Galaxy S25 running smoothly, optimizing its performance regularly can help prevent slowdowns and glitches. One of the most effective ways to achieve this is by using the Device Care tool. This built-in feature helps you manage your device's storage, memory, battery, and security. It scans your phone for minor issues and fixes them before they start affecting the phone's speed and efficiency. By running the optimization process, you free up RAM, clear out temporary files, and identify any system issues. It's essentially a quick tune-up that helps maintain your device's peak performance. For optimal results, it's recommended to run Device Care at least once a week to keep your phone in top shape.

Managing background apps is another essential step in maintaining your phone's speed. Many apps, even when you're not actively using them, continue running in the background and consume valuable system resources like RAM and battery. These apps can unknowingly slow down your phone. To prevent this, regularly check and close background apps. You can do this through the Settings app by accessing Battery and Device Care, then tapping on Memory, and selecting Clean Now. Alternatively, you can manually close running apps by accessing the Recent Apps screen and swiping away the apps you're not using. For more control, you can go into the app settings and restrict battery usage for apps that aren't crucial, which will help conserve both battery and system resources.

Another important step is to manage your device's storage. If your phone runs low on storage, it can directly affect its speed and responsiveness. To free up space, go to Device Care in your Settings and check what's taking up the most space. Deleting unused apps, large files, and old downloads can immediately free up storage. Additionally, using Samsung's built-in storage optimizer to remove junk files can make a big difference. If you need more space, consider using cloud storage, moving apps to an SD card, or regularly clearing cache files. Keeping your storage organized helps your phone run more efficiently and prevents it from getting bogged down by unnecessary data.

Battery performance is also a key factor in keeping your phone running smoothly. As batteries age, they can contribute to slower performance and shorter battery life. To optimize battery usage, enable Adaptive Battery in your Settings under Battery and Device Care. This feature helps prioritize power for apps you use most frequently. You can also toggle between different performance modes, such as Optimized Mode for balanced performance or Power Saving Mode for longer battery life. If your battery drains quickly, you can check the Battery Usage section in your Settings to see which apps are consuming the most power.

Software and app updates are crucial for keeping your Galaxy S25 Ultra running at its best. These updates often include performance improvements, bug fixes, and security patches that can help optimize your device's functionality. To ensure your device stays up to date, go to Settings, tap Software Update, and select Download and Install. Don't forget to update your apps as well, which you can do through the Google Play Store. Enabling automatic updates for both your device's software and apps is a great way to ensure you never miss an important update.

Managing overheating is essential for preventing thermal throttling, which occurs when your device gets too hot and slows down to avoid damage. Overheating can be caused by using your phone in direct sunlight, running intensive apps like gaming or video streaming, or using features like 5G and Bluetooth when they aren't necessary. To keep your phone cool, avoid using it in hot environments, close heavy apps when not in use, and disable unnecessary features. Samsung's Temperature Protection Mode is another great option to help prevent overheating, and switching to a slim, heat-dissipating case can also make a significant difference.

Auto Settings

To ensure your Galaxy S25 maintains optimal performance without having to manually intervene, you can enable automatic optimization settings that help keep your device running smoothly throughout the day. These auto settings work in the background, freeing you from having to remember to optimize or restart your phone.

To get started, first, open the Settings app on your device. From the menu, go to the Device Care section, where you'll find tools for managing your device's performance. Once you're in the Device Care section, tap on the More options icon, and then select Advanced to access further settings.

Within the Advanced settings, you'll find several options to optimize your phone automatically. To keep everything running smoothly without manual effort, you can activate the Auto optimization feature. This ensures that your phone is automatically optimized once a day, which includes clearing unnecessary files and closing background apps to free up resources and improve overall performance.

You can also activate the Auto restart feature. This allows your device to restart automatically at a set time, helping refresh the system and clear out any temporary files or memory usage that might be slowing down your device.

Finally, the Optimise settings feature helps conserve battery by adjusting your device's settings when it's not in use. For instance, when your phone is idle, it can automatically make adjustments that help reduce power consumption, ensuring you get the most out of your battery.

By enabling these auto settings, you can ensure that your device is consistently running at its best without needing to remember to perform routine optimizations. These features will help your Galaxy S25 continue to perform efficiently, with minimal effort on your part.

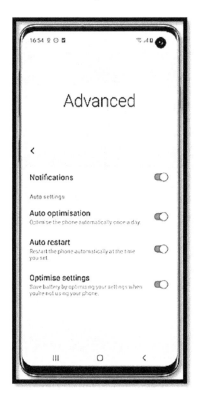

MANAGING STORAGE AND BACKUPS

Clear Storage

Managing storage is essential to maintaining its performance and responsiveness. Over time, your phone can accumulate unused apps, large files, and other data that can take up valuable space, which can ultimately slow down your device. To ensure that your phone continues to run smoothly, it's important to regularly review and delete unnecessary files.

One of the simplest ways to free up space is by deleting unused apps and old documents. Start by opening the Settings app on your device. From there, navigate to Device Care, where you'll find the Storage section. This section gives you a detailed overview of how your storage is being used and which types of files are occupying the most space.

Once you're in the Storage section, you can choose to examine different categories of files, such as Documents, Images, or other types of data that may be cluttering your device. By tapping on each category, you can see a list of the files within it. If there are items you no longer need, simply select them for deletion.

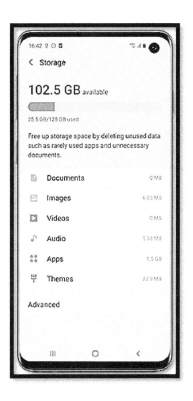

After selecting the items you wish to remove, tap Delete, and then confirm the deletion by tapping Delete again. This will free up valuable space on your phone, improving its speed and responsiveness. Remember, regularly cleaning out your device can prevent unnecessary files from slowing it down and keep it running at optimal performance.

This process is simple but effective in maintaining the overall health of your device. By taking the time to clear out unused data, you ensure that your phone remains efficient and that storage space is used only for the things that matter most to you.

Clean the Memory

When you use your Galaxy S25 regularly, it's common for apps and processes to run in the background, consuming memory and slowing down the overall performance of the device. Memory is crucial for the fast loading of apps, switching between tasks, and running games smoothly. If you've noticed that your device is becoming sluggish or apps aren't functioning as they should, it's often because the memory is filled with unnecessary background processes. Freeing up memory by closing these apps can help your phone return to its optimal speed.

To start, head over to the Settings app on your phone, where you'll find the Device Care section. This is where you can manage various aspects of your device, including memory. Once you're in the Device Care menu, tap on the Memory option. Here, you'll see an overview of memory usage, and it will highlight which apps or processes are consuming the most resources.

If you have specific apps that you don't want to include in the cleaning process, you can customize the memory cleaning feature. Tap on Apps to exclude from cleaning, then select Add Apps. From there, you can pick the apps you want to exclude from being cleared during this process, which gives you more control over what gets cleaned.

Once you're ready to free up memory, simply tap on Clean Now. The system will begin to close unnecessary background apps and processes, clearing up memory to improve performance. This simple action can help your device run faster, with apps and games functioning smoothly once again.

Regularly cleaning out the memory in this way ensures that your device maintains the speed and efficiency you expect, preventing slowdowns and ensuring that your apps operate properly.

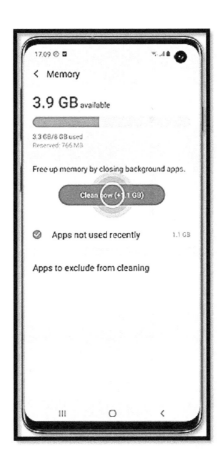

Back up with Samsung Account

For you to ensure that all your important data is securely backed up, start by navigating to the Settings menu on your device. Once you're in the settings, look for the Accounts and Backup section. Within this section, you'll find the Samsung Cloud option, which allows you to back up various types of data such as apps, contacts, photos, and more.

When you tap on Samsung Cloud, you'll be directed to the Backup data option. This feature allows you to choose which types of data you want to back up, such as app data, system settings, or media files.

Once you've selected the data you want to back up, simply tap the Back up now button. The time it takes to complete the backup will depend on the amount of data you're saving, but you can expect it to take just a few minutes.

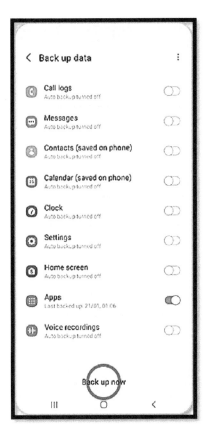

After the backup is complete, you'll see a confirmation message, and you can tap Done to exit the process. It's always a good idea to back up your data regularly, especially before making any changes to your device or performing system updates.

Restoring your data from a backup is also simple, especially if you need to transfer your information to a new device. If you're using a Samsung account to back up your data, you can follow these steps to restore it. Open Settings, go back to Accounts and Backup, and then tap on Restore data under Samsung Cloud. If you have multiple devices backed up to the same Samsung account, you will see a list of all your backups. Choose the backup you wish to restore from, and then select the apps and data you want to bring back to your device.

Once you've made your selections, tap Restore to begin the process. If prompted, tap Install to ensure that your apps and home screen settings are restored as well. This feature ensures that your apps and data will be set up just as they were on your previous device, allowing for a smooth transition without losing important information.

Back up or restore with a Google Account

Backing up your important data to Google Drive, you will first need to access your device's Settings menu. Once you're in the settings, look for the Accounts and Backup section. This area contains various options related to managing your accounts and backing up your data, including the option for backing up your information to Google Drive.

Next, under Google Drive, you will find the option to Back up data. Tapping on this will give you access to settings where you can choose which data you would like to back up, such as app data, contacts, calendar events, and more.

Once you've selected the appropriate data you want to back up, tap **Back up now** to begin the backup process.

The amount of time it takes for the backup to complete will depend on the amount of data being saved, but it should only take a few moments. This feature helps ensure that your important information is stored safely in the cloud, allowing you to restore it to a new device or recover it in case anything happens to your current one. Once the backup is complete, your data will be securely stored in your Google Drive account and ready to be accessed when needed.

SOFTWARE UPDATES AND SECURITY PATCHES

User-Initiated Software Update

You need to manually check for available updates by navigating through the settings. First, from your home screen, swipe up or down to access the full list of apps. From there, tap on the Settings app and then select System Updates from the available options. Once you're in the System Updates section, choose Check for System Updates to see if there's any new software available for your device.

If an update is available, you will see a prompt to Download now. Tap on this option to begin the download. The speed of the download will depend on your internet connection, so it may take a few moments. Once the download is complete, a notification will appear informing you that the update is ready to be installed. At this point, tap Install Update to begin the installation process.

During installation, your device will automatically power down and then reboot. This is a standard procedure that allows the new software to be properly integrated into your system. Once the update is complete, the device will power on, and you will see a message confirming that the installation has finished successfully. At this stage, you can tap OK to exit the process.

After the update, your device will be running the latest version of the software, ensuring you have the most recent features, security patches, and performance improvements. It's a simple yet crucial process to keep your device functioning at its best.

Wi-Fi Only OTA Programming - Wi-Fi Exclusive Update

When Wi-Fi is turned on and your device is connected to a Wi-Fi network, it can automatically receive and download new software updates. The update process will continue even if the Wi-Fi connection is interrupted, allowing you to switch between multiple Wi-Fi networks without losing progress. The device will resume downloading the update from where it left off each time it reconnects to a Wi-Fi network, ensuring a seamless experience.

Once the download is finished, your device will notify you that a new software update is ready for installation. To proceed, simply tap Install Now, and the device will begin the installation process. It will power down, reboot, and start applying the new update. After the installation is complete, the update will be successfully installed, and your device will be running the latest version of the software, which may include new features, improvements, and security patches.

Server- Initiated Software Update

When a software update becomes available, your device will notify you, prompting you to take action. Upon receiving the notification, you can select Install Now, which will begin the update process. Your device will power down and then restart as it installs the update. Once it's ready, you will be asked to tap OK to confirm the start of the installation.

If you prefer to delay the installation, you have the option to choose Defer, which will push the update installation to a later time. After deferring, you will be returned to the Home screen, and the software update notification will continue to appear periodically until you decide to install it.

Should you wish to manually initiate the update at any point after receiving the first notification, simply navigate to the Home screen, then open Applications and go to Settings. From there, tap About Device, followed by Software Updates. In the System Updates section, you can tap Restart & install to start the update. This will cause your device to power off and restart to begin the installation process.

Once the update is successfully installed, the device will restart once more, and the new software will be fully applied, ensuring your device is up-to-date with the latest improvements and features.

System Update while Roaming

You need to know that when you want to update your system through roaming, your device won't notify you about available software updates. This is because updates are typically restricted to stable network connections, which may not be available while roaming. However, there are still ways to update your device.

One option is to connect to a Wi-Fi network. Once connected, the update notice should appear, allowing you to proceed with the installation. Alternatively, if you want to manually check for updates while roaming, you can navigate to the Home screen, open Applications, and go to Settings. From there, select About device, followed by Software Updates to check for any available updates.

If you're not connected to Wi-Fi, you will need to enable it by going to Settings, selecting Wireless & networks, and then tapping on Wi-Fi. You can either choose an available Wi-Fi network or manually add one to connect. Once connected, your device will be able to receive the update notification.

If the software update fails to install, an error screen will appear. This doesn't mean that your device is damaged; it simply indicates that the installation wasn't completed. The device will restart, returning to the original software, and the update notification will prompt you again.

If the Wi-Fi connection is weak or unstable, the software update may not be successful over the air. In such cases, a more reliable option is to connect your device to a computer with an active internet connection. By using a USB cable, connect your phone to the computer and download the Software Upgrade Assistant tool. This tool will check for any software updates and allow you to initiate the update process through your computer instead of the mobile network. This method ensures a stable and secure connection for the software update to be completed successfully.

Cleaning and Physical Care Tips

Before you start up the cleaning process, ensure that your device is turned off and disconnected from any power sources. Remove any cases, covers, or accessories that may be attached to the device to ensure a thorough cleaning.

A microfiber cloth, which is soft and lint-free, is the best option for cleaning your device. Alternatively, a camera lens cleaning cloth can be used as well. These types of clothes are gentle enough to avoid causing any damage to the device while effectively removing dirt, smudges, and fingerprints. Gently wipe the front and back of your device with the microfiber cloth, ensuring that you do not press too hard, as excessive pressure can cause scratches or damage.

Be cautious not to apply excess moisture to your device. If necessary, you can lightly dampen the corner of the microfiber cloth with distilled water to address more stubborn dirt or grime. Avoid allowing any liquid to seep into the device, as moisture can damage internal components.

For disinfecting purposes, you can use a disinfectant solution, such as one based on hypochlorous acid or alcohol (containing 50-80ppm or over 70% ethanol or isopropyl alcohol). However, never apply the disinfectant directly to the device. Instead, lightly dampen the microfiber cloth with the solution, ensuring that it is not soaking wet, and gently wipe down the device. This method helps avoid any potential harm that could come from liquid seeping into the device's openings.

It is important to avoid using compressed air cans for cleaning, as they may cause damage to the device's surface. Additionally, refrain from using spray bleach or any harsh chemicals, as these can be too abrasive and potentially cause damage to both the appearance and functionality of your device. Always prioritize gentle cleaning methods to maintain the integrity of your device.

CHAPTER 10

ADVANCED FEATURES AND TIPS

USING BIXBY VOICE ASSISTANT

Use the side to activate the Bixby

Access your apps by swiping them up from the home screen.

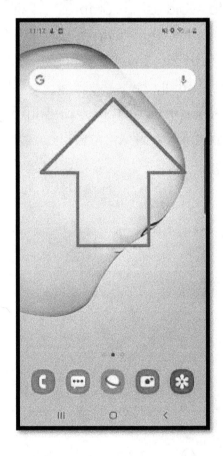

Once you are in the apps section, open the Settings app.

After opening Settings, navigate to Advanced Features and select it.

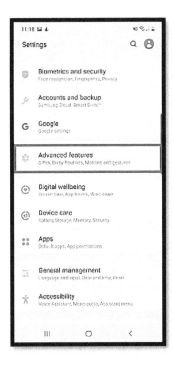

From there, tap the Side key to customize the button's functionality.

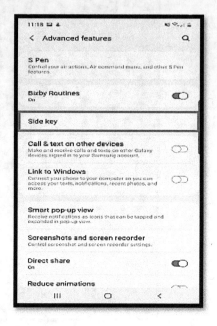

If you'd like to use Bixby with a double press of the side button, ensure the Open Bixby option is selected. In case this option is not visible, enable the double-press feature by tapping the switch next to it. Once the option appears, tap Open Bixby.

If you prefer using Bixby by holding the side key, activate the Wake Bixby feature. This allows you to launch Bixby by simply holding the side key for a moment, giving you an efficient way to use Bixby hands-free.

Sitting up Bixby

Activate Bixby by pressing either the Bixby key or the side key on your device.

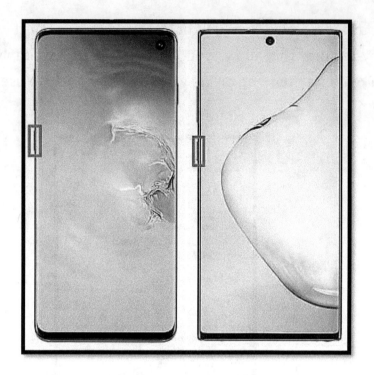

Once Bixby is activated, you will be guided through the setup process.

If you are not already signed in to your Samsung account, you will be prompted to log in. After signing in, you will need to review and agree to the terms and conditions.

Once you've read the terms and conditions, tap the checkbox to indicate your acceptance. Afterward, proceed by tapping the next icon to continue with the setup process.

Resetting Bixby

If you're experiencing issues with Bixby not recognizing your voice or not performing as expected, resetting Bixby can often resolve these problems. Since Bixby's features are divided into different apps, it's easy to reset the specific feature causing trouble.

Start by swiping up on your home screen to access your apps.

From there, open the Settings app.

Once in the Settings menu, scroll down and tap Apps.

In the Apps section, locate and select Bixby Voice.

After tapping on Bixby Voice, go to Storage.

Here, you will see the option to Clear data.

Tapping this will reset the app, clearing any data that may be causing issues, and allowing you to set it up again, then tap ok.

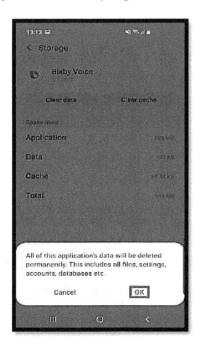

Use the Bixby Key to open an App

Swipe up from the home screen to bring up your apps.

Open the Settings app and then navigate to Advanced Features. Tap on the Bixby key, where you will find the option to set up or customize how you want to activate Bixby.

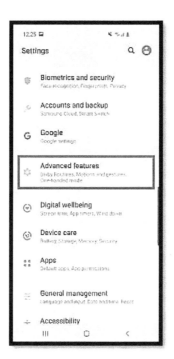

If you haven't already set up Bixby, you'll be prompted to tap Get Started to begin the setup process.

Afterward, you can choose whether you'd like to activate Bixby with a single press or a double press of the Bixby key. Based on your preference, you can assign the Bixby key to either open an app or run a specific command.

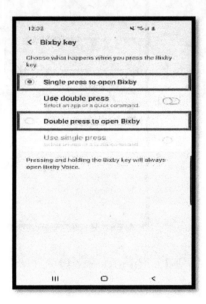

If you select the option to activate an app or command, tap the switch to enable this feature.

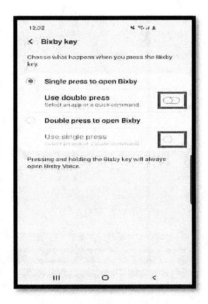

You can then choose whether to open an app or execute a quick command when you press the Bixby key.

If you choose to open an app, select the app you want to launch with the Bixby key.

Alternatively, if you decide to run a quick command, tap the specific command you wish to activate using the Bixby key. This customization allows you to streamline your experience and make Bixby even more efficient for your needs.

MULTI-WINDOW AND SPLIT-SCREEN FUNCTIONS

Split Screen Apps

The split screen feature on your device allows you to use two apps at the same time, giving you the ability to multitask efficiently. This is especially useful if you regularly use two apps simultaneously. For instance, you can easily browse the web while checking your messages or emails without switching back and forth between screens.

To begin, swipe left from the right side of the Home screen to bring up the Multi window tray, where you can see a list of apps you currently have open. Tap the grid at the bottom of the screen to access all of your apps. From here, drag and drop one app into the top or bottom portion of the screen to begin using it in split screen view. After that, repeat the same action with the second app to complete the setup.

Alternatively, you can also use the Recents button. Once you're in the Recents view, tap an app's icon at the top of the screen and choose either Open in split screen view or Open in pop-up view. This gives you even more flexibility in arranging your apps.

While in split screen mode, you can adjust the size of each app's window by dragging the blue divider between them. This allows you to customize how much space each app takes up, depending on what you're doing. For example, you might want a larger window for reading emails and a smaller one for browsing the web.

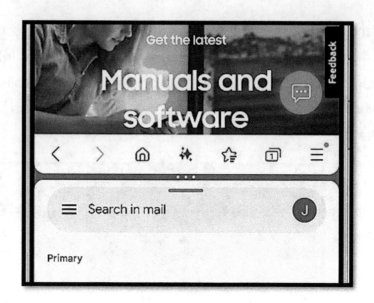

If you often use the same pair of apps together, you can create an app pair for quick access. In the Recents screen, swipe to find the apps you want to pair together, tap the app's icon at the top of the screen, and select Add app pair. From there, you can choose where you want the apps to appear on the screen.

If you want to close one of the apps in a split screen or pop-up view, simply tap the blue divider at the top of the screen and hit the **X** icon. This will remove the app from the screen, leaving the other app open and active.

Separate App Sound

You can enjoy media sounds from your favorite apps using a different audio device, offering a more customized listening experience. The process begins by accessing the Settings on your phone and tapping on Sounds and Vibration. From there, you'll find the option labeled Separate app sound. Activate this feature by tapping the switch next to Turn on now. Once the feature is enabled, you'll be prompted to select the apps that you want to play on a different audio device. This allows you to choose specific apps for audio redirection, giving you full control over which apps use which audio device.

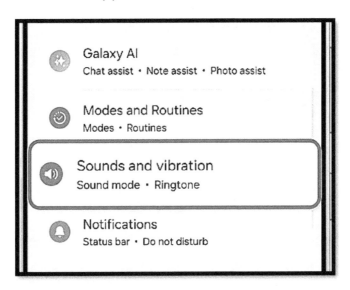

After selecting the apps, you can tap Add Apps if you want to add more apps to this list. Once you're done, tap Back to proceed. The next step is to choose the audio device where the selected apps will play their sounds. You'll have the option to select either your phone's internal speaker or a connected Bluetooth device. Keep in mind that the Bluetooth option will only appear if a Bluetooth device is already paired with your phone.

After selecting the audio device, tap Back again, and your chosen apps will start playing their sounds on the selected device. If you want to change the apps or audio device later on, you can return to Separate app sound in the Settings and make adjustments. To fine-tune the volume of each app, simply press the volume button. A pop-up menu will appear showing the volume levels and the current sound type. By tapping the three horizontal dots at the top of the pop-up, you can expand the menu and adjust the volume sliders for each app to your liking. This allows for a highly personalized audio setup across your apps and devices.

INDEX

V	W
Video mode, 96, 97	widget, 4, 53, 54, 56, 57, 62
Voice commands, 94, 109	Wi-Fi, 5, 7, 13, 15, 18, 22, 64, 78,
Volume buttons, 94, 109	79, 80, 82, 130, 131, 136, 137,
	139, 142, 159, 161, 162